Under the Nazi Heel

The Eastern Front, Book 2

By Scott Bury

Under the Nazi Heel
Copyright 2016 by Scott Bury
All rights reserved

No part of this story may be used or reproduced in any manner without the prior written permission of the author, except for brief quotations in reviews.

Cover design by David C. Cassidy

Edited by Joy Lorton, Typo-Detective

Quality control by iAi Independent Authors International

Published by The Written Word Communications Company, Ottawa, Ontario, Canada

www.writtenword.ca

ISBN 978-1-987846-02-7

Under the Nazi Heel

The Eastern Front, Book 2

By Scott Bury

IN MEMORY OF MAURICE BURY

Dedicated to Roxanne

Under the Nazi Heel is the second volume recounting the World War 2 experience of Canadian Maurice Bury. The story begins with *Army of Worn Soles*, which you can find on Amazon, ASIN B00L3CNE0M.

Books by Scott Bury

Sam, the Strawb Part

Dark Clouds

Initiation Rites (The Bones of the Earth, Part 1)

The Bones of the Earth (The Dark Age, Book 1)

One Shade of Red

Walking Out of War series:

- *Army of Worn Soles*
- *Under the Nazi Heel*

Kindle World titles:

- *Torn Roots: A Lei Crime Kindle World mystery*
- *Jet: Stealth — A JET Kindle World adventure*
- *Palm Trees & Snowflakes: A Lei Crime Kindle World mystery*
- *The Wife Line: A Sydney Rye Kindle World mystery*

Find them all on Scott Bury's website, writtenword.ca

Contents

Prologue 8

Chapter 1: Back home 13

Chapter 2: New Year's Eve 25

Chapter 3: Recruited 35

Chapter 4: Tekla and the spy 40

Chapter 5: The jumper 45

Chapter 6: Intelligence 55

Chapter 7: Re-routing trains 64

Chapter 8: Slawko Kuritsa 75

Chapter 9: Night raid 79

Chapter 10: The heel grinds 91

Chapter 11: Meeting in the snow 100

Chapter 12: Kalush 111

Chapter 13: The battle of Ternopyl 127

Chapter 14: Changing occupiers 131

Chapter 15: The plot foiled 137

Chapter 16: Nightmare journey 146

Chapter 17: The Red Army 155

Preview from Walking Out of War 161

Acknowledgements 165

About the author 166

Prologue

Volhynia, Ukraine, February 1943

Wind blew the snow smooth, polishing the surface of the lake to a dull sheen under the full moon, and pushing drifts higher than a man along a rough fence that shielded the railway. Beyond the rails, more snow weighed down the boughs of close-growing fir trees and covered their trunks more than six feet high.

The moonlight made steam sparkle as a train puffed and groaned from the forest slowly along the edge of the frozen lake, the lantern mounted on its front a second moon. The engineer squinted through the small forward window, which gave only an obstructed view. Periodically, he leaned out the side window to peer at the track ahead, but he could only bear the frigid air, the wind from the train's forward motion, and the smoke and cinders from the engine, for less than a minute before he had to come back inside.

He kept the train's speed low and one hand on the brake lever, despite the commands of the Wehrmacht officers in the cars behind him. He knew the risks of going too fast in this country. Even though snowplows were welded to the front of the engine, snow drifts over the tracks could derail the train. And besides that, he knew men hidden under the dark boughs posed a worse threat.

Beyond the frozen lake, the forest fell back from the tracks to open fields on each side. A thin layer of snow had drifted over the fences and covered the tracks since the day-crews had cleared them. The plow on the front of the engine pushed the snow away. Still, the engineer turned a valve and slowed the train even more. "No more fuel for now," he told the fireman behind him, without turning.

The engineer leaned out the side window again to squint forward. A shadow lay across the tracks ahead, where the forest converged again on the railroad. He blinked and peered one more time to confirm his fear. He pulled inside and put all his weight onto the brake lever. "Ring the alarm!" he shouted to the fireman.

The steel brakes screamed and threw the engineer and fireman to the front of the cabin, pressing them against the hot iron. The engineer spun valves to release pressure. Clouds of steam whistled out of a dozen places on the engine and bells rang in every car.

The train slowed but the momentum of the passenger cars pushed the engine until it rammed a barricade of trees that had been felled over the tracks where they slipped into the forest again. The logs cracked with a noise like exploding gunpowder. Some flew off the tracks, sending up tidal waves of snow when they came down again. One hit the lantern, extinguishing its yellow light. Others rolled forward on the tracks only to be caught again as the train continued, slowing. They wedged under the engine. It shuddered. Its metal voice screamed in pain. It tilted, threatening to tip over. The engine left the track, sending waves of drifted snow over the fields.

The passenger cars slammed successively into the rear of the coal car, pushing the engine farther. It dug a long trench, sending more snow into the air. Finally, the train groaned to a stop. For minutes, the scene resembled a moonlit blizzard as the disturbed snow fell a second time.

Steam hissed from the engine, the fire in its furnace rumbled, bells clamoured the length of the train, and cries and moans of the passengers echoed across the fields and lake. A door on a passenger car creaked open and clanged as it hit the bent side of the car.

The wind sighed through the boughs of the fir trees, shaking snowflakes to spiral down. Nothing else moved in the clearing or on the lake. The whistling of steam grew lower and softer. The fire in the furnace became silent.

Minutes passed. Only the steam moved from the broken engine, driven by the gentle wind.

Finally, a helmeted head poked out of the one open door and withdrew immediately. After another minute, the head reappeared and looked left and right. More steam came from his mouth. A muffled order from behind, and the soldier jumped out of the car, struggling to keep his submachine gun above the snow as he sank to his waist. Another followed him, pointing a submachine gun into the darkness beyond the moonlight.

A third soldier jumped out and struggled to move forward, toward the engine. Another soldier jumped out behind him and started to stomp down the snow under the door, to make a slightly clearer area, and then followed the third soldier forward, widening the path he had begun.

Finally, a junior officer in a peaked cap and long coat, holding a pistol in his hand, jumped into the cleared area. He lifted his gloved hands to his mouth and breathed on them in a vain attempt to warm them.

The two soldiers had nearly reached the engine by that time and they called out to the engineer in German. They heard no answer.

The officer ordered one of the men in the snow with him to clear him a path to the next car. He followed the soldier until he could bang on the side of the second passenger car with the butt of his pistol. After a few seconds, that door opened slowly and another junior officer climbed down.

Down the train, doors opened in every passenger car and soldiers and officers climbed out. Men asked "What happened? Why did the train derail? What happened to the engineer?" Officers asked "Any injuries? No? Weapons ready?" Soldiers formed a defensive line, weapons pointed into the forest or toward the lake, but they had trouble holding their rifles and machine guns over the top of the snow.

At the engine, the first two soldiers to come out of the train began to climb the ladder to the engineer's compartment. The first soldier knocked on the door.

He was answered by a rifle shot from the forest. He arched his back and fell into the snow, knocking the man below him down.

More rifle shots came from the forest, hitting the officers first, then the soldiers with submachine guns. The Germans returned fire blindly. They could not see their attackers and their bullets went uselessly into the trees.

Fire came at the Germans from all sides. Some of the men in the snow tried to climb back into the train but they were cut down, shot in the back. The moonlight turned the blood black on the snow.

A burning torch flew out of the forest, turning end over end to land on top of the first passenger car. Made of steel, it did not burn. But more torches flew, aimed toward the open doors. Most bounced off the sides of the cars and fell into the snow, snuffed.

Then an explosion blew off the rear of the last car and the Germans knew their attackers had grenades. They tried to hide between the cars or under the snow, but one by one they fell. More explosions came from under the train, and then someone managed to pitch a grenade into one of the doors. Smoke followed the muffled bang. Within a minute the men outside could see flames, and they knew they were dead.

One soldier fired his submachine gun in controlled bursts from a hiding spot between two of the cars, but bullets found him. Before his body hit the snow, a comrade took the gun from him and fired a continuous volley into the woods until he was hit three times from different directions.

Beside him, the junior officer who had tried to warm his hands fell with a bullet in his upper thigh. Blood gushing into his long coat, he raised his pistol to his head and blew his brains out before the partisans could take him.

The whole train was ablaze by then. Soldiers jumped out through windows and doors to be killed by more bullets. Within minutes, it was over. All the men outside the train lay dead in the snow, while those in the train screamed as they burned.

Under the trees, men in black uniforms watched carefully. One man shot a German body, just to be sure he was dead, and then the insurgents stood up. In twos and threes, they got into sleighs hidden in the woods, slapped the reins and returned along the paths they had made when they had arrived, hours earlier.

The only sound was the muffled steps of their horses in the snow and the soft roar of the fire, and soon only the fire was left.

The Ukrainian Insurgent Army had begun operations against the occupying Germans.

Chapter 1: Back home

Ternopyl, December 1941

A rooster crowed and Maurice bolted up in bed, wondering where he was. *Where is the bugle?*

He looked side to side without recognizing where he was. It seemed familiar, but where were his men? His uniform? His pistol?

He saw the window, the grey sky beyond. The red and orange horizon. It was morning. He saw his dresser, his bed.

His bed.

Not the army's bed.

He fell back onto the mattress, looking at the familiar ceiling. *What time is it?*

Memory came back. He was home. Safe. In his mother's house, in his own bed, the bed he hadn't seen in — what? Nine months?

He felt weight on his eyelids. *Just a few minutes, that's all. Then I'll get up.*

He woke hours later. It had been the first good night's sleep he'd had in months, since before he had left to join the army. The months now seemed like an entire lifetime. His familiar bedroom looked strange, foreign in some way he could not define.

He looked in the mirror, surprised to see the man looking back at him. He realized that he had always thought of himself as handsome. High cheekbones, a straight nose, hazel eyes under a wave in his thick brown hair. But now that hair hung limp and ragged, his eyes looked dull with dark semi-circles sagging below them. His cheeks were dark hollows. Lines cracked his lips and coarse stubble grew in thin patches across his jaw and throat.

I look like I crawled out of hell. I guess I did.

An aroma reached his nose, an odour he hadn't sensed in months. Immediately, his mouth got wet and his stomach growled. Mama's cooking. He found his old housecoat in the wardrobe and pulled it on as he nearly ran down to the kitchen.

Somehow, his mother had managed to gather enough food to put a magnificent breakfast on the table: sausages, eggs, kasha and tea. She cried as she put the dishes in front of him. "Maurice, you're so thin, so thin. What did they do to you?"

Maurice could only manage a few bites. "Delicious, Mama. I haven't eaten food like this since … I've missed you so much." He stood so his mother could embrace him.

She pulled away to wipe tears from her face. "But why don't you eat more? Please, Merosho," she said, using her pet name for him. She put a plate of homemade bread, sliced thick, in front of him.

The food was delicious, but Maurice just could not swallow another bite. His stomach had shrunk.

"I'm sorry, Mama. I just can't. Maybe later." He sat again to sip his tea. If only there was a slice of lemon to put in it, but lemons hadn't been available since 1939, when the Soviet Union occupied western Ukraine.

Later, his mother and sister sat with him in the kitchen as the thin winter sunlight crept across the floor. They told him what had happened since the Soviet Army had drafted him the previous April, and especially since the Germans invaded on June 22.

"We welcomed them in," said his sister, Hanya. "In some of the villages near the border—the new border after 1939, when the Russians came—girls gave flowers to the German soldiers. The village elders even brought the traditional bread and salt. The Germans were pushing out the Communists. So we thought. And they brought thousands of leaflets and newspapers saying 'Freedom to all nations.'"

"Freedom from the Communists and the Russians," his mother nodded. "They opened the churches, too."

"Yes, they've let us have our religion again," Hanya agreed. "And that's been a great comfort to us. And in June, Stepan Bandera and the Organization of Ukrainian Nationals announced an independent government for Ukraine."

Maurice was shocked. "Independent Ukraine? The Germans permitted this?"

Hanya nodded. "For about a week. Then the Gestapo arrested Bandera and Melnyk and the prime minister, Stetsko. The Germans call this part of Ukraine 'Galicia' now."

"Halychyna," said his mother with a little smile.

"No, mama, not Halychyna," Hanya corrected her. "That's our name for this province. Fritz calls it Galicia, like the Austro-Hungarian Empire did." Maurice nodded. The Germans were continuing the policy of all the old colonizers: the Soviets, the Russians, the Austrians, the Pole and Lithuanians: they barely admitted that Ukraine was anything but empty land, waiting for them to civilize it.

Later, Maurice walked to the village to look for friends, or anyone he knew who might have evaded the Soviets and the Germans. His old coat and boots were loose because he had lost weight in the German prison camp. Even his hat seemed to slip lower on his head.

There were no young men on the street or in the market on that cold December day. Carts had dug deep ruts through the snow, and Maurice walked along them to Komorski's place, which passed for a café in the village. It was a small yellow house with a wide porch. In summer, Komorski would put two little tables and a few chairs for people to sit. It was inconceivable that the café, a little shop in a tiny village in western Ukraine, would actually have coffee. But it was still a gathering place for the locals, who would gossip while nibbling Mrs. Komorski's biscuits and drinking tea brewed from dried local herbs, or the vodka and whiskey that Komorski distilled at night.

In December, no one was sitting outside, but inside was a man that Maurice knew: Vasyl, the village loafer. He wasn't that old, but for years he could almost always be found at the café. His farm was a tiny plot, which he rented out to one neighbour or another to grow a few cash crops on. His wife subsisted on selling eggs and taking in laundry for wealthier households, and Vasyl whiled away the days at the café, bumming cigarettes, newspapers and cups of tea, and giving a remarkably salient political discussion in return.

Vasyl goggled when Maurice sat down beside him. "Maurice Bury! You really are alive. I heard there was a big party at your mother's place last night, but I didn't believe that you had really come back from home. We heard you were dead. Why, it was Myhasch Hrynyki—you know, from the big farm across the river—he said he saw you dead with his own eyes. Oh, how your poor mother cried."

Maurice pulled off his coat, hat and scarf, shaking the cold off his body. Komorski's house had always been drafty, and now it seemed worse than usual.

Komorski came from somewhere in the back. "Maurice Bury? Tekla Kuritsa's son?" He grabbed Maurice by the shoulders. "I almost didn't recognize you." He kissed Maurice on both cheeks and then leaned back, hands still on Maurice's shoulders. "Well, it's no wonder—how much weight have you lost, son?"

Komorski was a small, thin man with a balding pink head and a tiny, neat goatee. He had delicate, quick hands suited to making glasses of tea and slicing bread, and he moved in nervous, fast spurts.

Maurice knew Komorski only slightly; his mother could not be bothered with going to a shop to drink tea when she had her own at home. "I don't know," he answered.

"You look like a little boy in your daddy's clothes." Komorski said. "Just wait, I'll get you a cup of tea and something to eat. Don't you worry—it's on the house today." He bustled to the back of the house.

"And something for me, too?" said Vasyl. Komorski waved one hand in a dismissive gesture.

"My God, it's good to see you, Maurice," Vasyl said as he tugged his threadbare coat closer around his shoulders. "I almost cry when I think of all the young men who've been taken away from this village. So many lost. And we don't even know for certain what's happened to most of them, whether they're alive or dead."

"So all the young men were drafted?" Drafting every man of fighting age would fit the communists' philosophy.

"Not all—the communists just aren't that organized. You know the Russians!" he guffawed, but became serious again almost immediately. "No, the Russians didn't take everyone. They took you, and Bohdan Melnyk from down the old road, Ihor Terminsky from his farm, those three young boys who were always together, Danilo, Mekolya and Roman, young Taras Pavlenko from Mykulynicki, you know the boy who was in love with Nadia Premenchuk, many, many more. But the Germans took even more young men away. Sent them to work on farms in Silesia or God knows where else. They took some mechanics and others, too, to work in factories. They say they're working on making guns and shells."

"How does anyone know this?"

Vasyl shrugged. "They took young girls, too, you know."

Maurice felt his heart pounding in his chest. "What for?"

"To be serving girls and God knows what else for rich Germans. Some are still in the area, working like slaves for German officers. Some have been turned into whores, poor things."

Maurice was getting tired of the loafer's rumours. "Is there a newspaper anywhere?"

Komorski returned carrying a tray with a teapot, three mugs and a bowl of little cookies. "These are the last my wife made this fall, Maurice. Not you, Vasyl, unless you want to start paying for your tea." He poured three cups and squeezed a thin lemon slice into each one. "We still have a few lemons, though, from before the Germans came. It wasn't easy hiding them from the German officers, let me tell you!"

Vasyl blew across his tea, eyes on the cookies. Maurice put one in his mouth: almost, but not quite as good as his mother's. After his months on army rations and weeks of starvation in the prison camp, they were delicious.

Komorski took a small bottle from his apron pocket and poured a measure of his home-brewed whiskey, samohanka, into Maurice's tea and his own. Vasyl pushed his cup toward the bottle, eyes begging. Komorski glared at him, then allowed a few drops into his cup, too. Maurice drank. The mixture of herb tea, whiskey and the aftertaste of the cookies was awful, but he drank more, anyway. Warmth spread through his body, across his shoulders and up his face. He drank again.

"Vasyl tells me the Germans took a lot of young people away," Maurice said. Komorski nodded. "Are they still doing that? Should I hide?"

"No, don't worry. They mostly took Ukrainians and Poles from Ternopyl, to work in factories or farms. But the Germans are busy with other things, now. They haven't taken anyone since the summer, unless they arrest them for stealing or getting political. You'll be safe enough, as long as you stay out of trouble."

"What constitutes trouble among the Germans?"

Komorski sat down and leaned close. "Politics. Nationalism," he said quietly. "How much did you hear when you were in the army?"

"Nothing. Just propaganda about how the Russians were repelling the invaders. Absolutely nothing about home."

Komorski took a long sip of his tea-whiskey. "A week after the invasion, Stepan Bandera and his faction of the OUN declared a free Ukrainian state with Yaroslav Stetsko as Prime Minister."

OUN, the Organization of Ukrainian Nationalists, had been working for a free Ukrainian nation since 1929. But it had split in 1940 between a conservative faction, headed by Andriy Melnyk, and the radical and violent Bandera.

Maurice nodded. "Hitler did promise 'freedom for all nations.'"

Komorski snorted. "More propaganda. The Ukrainian state lasted less than a week. The Gestapo arrested Bandera and Stetsko and all their friends and shot a bunch of other so-called Ukrainian government people. They also shot the Jews."

Maurice swallowed. "All the Jews? Non-combatants?"

"Not all, just the leaders. Then they roused up some local nitwits to kill about 500 of them at a cemetery.

You know Hitler's hatred for Jews. All over Poland, the SS rounds up the Jews and confines them to ghettos."

"And Bandera? Did they shoot him?"

"No. He's in prison in Germany, but he manages to get messages out occasionally."

"What about Melnyk?"

"He was arrested, too, but his group …"

"What?"

Komorski stood, looking out the window. "I better not say any more now."

So, Bandera, who admired Hitler, is now his prisoner. Strange. He was such a supporter of Nazi Germany, and now they've taken him prisoner.

He needed to find out more, but Komorski did not want to speak.

"Do you have any newspapers?" Maurice asked again.

Komorski brought a tattered old single broadsheet from behind his makeshift counter. "This is the Ternopyl paper from yesterday. But it's only the news the Germans approve, so it's nonsense."

Maurice took it and scanned the headlines: German advances in Russia; the imminent fall of Moscow and Leningrad; the coldest winter in history in Russia was hurting the Bolshevists more than the glorious Wehrmacht and Luftwaffe.

"Looks pretty accurate from what I know," Maurice said.

Komorski produced another broadsheet, this one printed in Russian. "Where did you get that?" Maurice asked.

Komorski shrugged. "I can't say. These things have a way of turning up."

Maurice read it as quickly as he could. "This is impossible. The Russians say they're holding the Germans back at Vyasma, but the Germans say they're in the suburbs of Moscow. How old is this?"

"What's the date on it?" Komorski said.

"First November. It's over a month ago."

Vasyl slipped a biscuit out of the bowl. Komorski tried to slap it out of his hand, but he dodged the shopkeeper and popped it in his mouth. Komorski shook his head. "Come back again another day, Maurice. There will be other newspapers."

Maurice's mother would not let him do any heavy work for weeks. Fortunately, in winter, there was relatively little to do around the farm. Maurice filled his days with small repairs around the house, sweeping snow away from the doors, feeding chickens and collecting eggs. He helped his mother with the cooking, but most of the time enjoyed the feeling of boredom. It was so much better than hiding from the Germans and the commissars all day.

On Sundays, they went to the little church, as much to meet and talk with their neighbours as to worship. Every few days, he would go back to Komorski's shop for tea and news. Komorski never revealed how he got hold of German, Polish and even Russian-language newspapers, but when he did, a small group of men would gather around the tables to try to sift out a few truths from the propaganda. In North Africa, General Rommel destroyed hundreds of British tanks near Tobruk. The Germans had advanced to the suburbs of Leningrad and Moscow, and had dug in to await the spring. It was only a matter of time before the USSR collapsed and the Germans would liberate Russia from communism, just as it had Ukraine, Poland, Lithuania, Latvia and Estonia.

A few of the men—it was all men, who drank Komorski's samohanka to warm up—amused each other by comparing the Russian and German newspapers. "The Red Army has had a huge victory at Klin, and predict victory over the fascists in days." They laughed.

"That is impossible," said another man, pointing to an article on the front page of the Russian newspaper. "The Russians say they are holding the invaders back at Vilnius but the Germans claim to be 20 miles from Moscow."

"What's the date on the Russian paper?"

"First December."

"That's weeks old. The Germans took Vilnius in—what, November?"

"The truth is somewhere in between," Maurice said.

"The Red Army has used troops on skis outside Moscow," said the first man, reading from the Russian paper. "The Germans are freezing and the Party predicts the defeat of the enemy is imminent."

One day in December, Komorski rushed from the back of his café, brandishing a new German-language newspaper. "America has declared war on Germany, Italy and Japan!"

"The US is taking the side of the USSR?" Maurice asked. It seemed impossible.

"Your enemy's enemy is your friend," said Vasyl, sipping someone else's drink.

Another day, Komorski spread the official, German-sanctioned and edited Ukrainian newspaper on the table, smoothed it out and gestured for the other men to gather round. "What good is that sheet?" one man growled.

Komorski held a finger in front of pursed lips and then opened the newspaper. Inside, between the folds, was a single printed sheet titled Free Ukraine. It was a newspaper printed in Kyiv by Andriy Melnyk's faction of the Ukrainian Nationalist Organization, OUN-M. Maurice glanced over his shoulder, out the window, nervous in case anyone was on the street. *Can we trust everyone in here?* Possession of the paper meant summary execution if the Germans discovered it.

Its contents were slightly more reliable than those of the Russian, German or approved Ukrainian newspapers, but Maurice knew it equally a propaganda piece. Still, he put more credence in its stories about the German advance stalling west of Leningrad and Moscow, and of the gas lines freezing in the mechanized *wehrmact*.

When there were no newspapers, the men at Komorski's would sip hot water and tell Maurice what had happened in their village when he was away in the army. "The Germans had it easy at first," Vasyl liked to say. "They didn't even bother sending an armed force here. Just two soldiers on a motorcycle with a sidecar. They took off the muffler so it made so much noise, everybody ran away."

"In some villages, girls brought flowers to the Germans," said Mykal Kolody, an older farmer, echoing Maurice's sister. "They said they were liberating Ukraine from the communists. OUN declared an independent Ukraine in June, with Melnyk as President. The Germans arrested the whole bunch two weeks later, including Bandera."

"They shot most of them on the spot," Komorski said.

"As if that weren't bad enough, that bastard Bandera has his men killing Melnyk's people," said Kolody.

"Melnyk's an old man, and OUN-M are a bunch of old men," said Ivan Husar, a thin young man, just 18, who always trembled when the door opened and fidgeted with cutlery as he drank tea. "OUN-B is taking action against Ukraine's enemies."

"OUN-M are getting results in Kyiv," Kolody retorted. "And they're focused on the real enemies, not killing other Ukrainians."

"Ukraine is no more free now than we were under Poland," said another old man, Babiak. Another Babiak,

Maurice thought. How many people here are named Babiak? "We're in the *generalgouvernement* now."

"We're better off than eastern Ukraine," said Komorski. "They're under the *Reichskommissariat*—direct military control by the SS. They're brutal."

"Don't you realize what *generalgouvernement* means?" old Babiak said. "We're part of Germany now. The re-established German Empire. They're going to start pushing us out to make room for more of them. Haven't you heard of '*lebensraum*'?"

The word chilled Maurice. He thought of Professor Posmychuk, the gentle teacher in Ternopyl who had sheltered him that night he had come home. "When the Germans win this war, they're going to get rid of the Ukrainians and the Jews."

"That's enough of the political talk for now," Komorski growled. "It's best not to spend too much time talking about these things."

Chapter 2:
New Year's Eve

Nastaciv, Ukraine, 1942

St. Nikolas' Day came, but there were no children in the Kuritsa home, and Maurice and his family did not exchange presents. Christmas Day, two weeks later than in the West, meant nearly a whole day in the freezing church, stamping feet and blowing on hands, greeting neighbours and exchanging news while the priest and the choir sang.

On January 13, Hanya dragged Maurice to a Malanka dance at the Prosvita community hall in Nastaciv.

"I don't really feel like celebrating," Maurice protested. Hanya grabbed his arm in both her hands and hauled him out of the chair he slumped in.

"We can't just spend the whole winter stuck like a couple of turnips in the ground," she said. "Come on, if I don't get out and do something a little bit cheerful, I'm going to lose my mind.

Malanka is Ukrainian for New Year's Eve, celebrated by tradition according to the old Julian calendar, which the Orthodox Church continued to follow.

Protesting, Maurice pulled on his coat, boots and hat and drove the buggy to the Prosvita hall. The Nazis tolerated Prosvita, the "Taras Shevchenko Ukrainian Reading Society," named after the 19th-century artist and poet who had woken Ukraine's national consciousness. Prosvita did things like organize concerts and dances in community halls, once closed under the Polish government, reopened by the Soviets—although the Communists had not allowed the name "Prosvita" to be used.

The Nazis tolerated Ukrainian culture more than the Poles had—but then, the Poles had never deported slaves.

Despite Hanya's intentions, Maurice felt even more depressed when he walked into the hall beside the church. The interior was so cold, the few attendees kept their coats on. He had never seen such a small Malanka gathering—no more than 30 people in a hall that could hold hundreds. Up on the stage were a fiddler and old man Koval with an accordion, playing and dancing and smiling in a way that convinced no one.

A circle of teenaged girls and two young married couples danced on the floor. The rest of the guests sat at long tables, trying to appear cheerful. They didn't fool Maurice, either.

"Is this all that's left?" he asked his sister.

"No. I guess most people are as big sticks-in-the-mud as you and are staying home," she replied, poking Maurice in the chest. Then her smile fell. "But a lot of young people are gone. The Russians took some, and the Germans have taken more. Especially girls. They like the youngest, prettiest ones."

Maurice bought vodka for himself and his sister and sat at a table already populated by four Babiak siblings: Ivan, Mike, Nadia and Maria. The boys, a little older than Maurice, were well on their way to drunk, and Maria, a short, plump girl whose black hair always reminded Maurice of a squirrel's tail, was clapping and swaying to the music as she sat on the wooden chair.

"Maurice! Good to see you," said Mike, the younger of the brothers. He was very short and his straight yellow hair always made Maurice wonder whether his father was also Maria's. "How'sh the leg?"

"Just fine. Both of them, in fact," Maurice said. "Why shouldn't they be?"

"I thought you were wounded."

"No, that was you," said Maurice. He glanced at his sister, who smiled. She knew Maurice and his sense of humour better than anyone. "But it was your head, not your leg, that you injured. Don't you remember?"

"No," Mike said, slowly. He looked at his brother, who looked equally confused.

"Well, of course, you wouldn't remember. That was quite a blow to the head. You were out for days, and when you came to, you kept raving about the Germans invading."

"But, Maurice ..." Mike protested.

A bang interrupted him and Maurice felt a hand slap his shoulder. "Bury, what are you doing, talking to the most boring people here?"

Maurice turned as Slawko Kuritsa dropped into the chair beside him. He banged a cup onto the table and vodka slopped over the rim. "Have a drink on me, war hero."

Slawko was a distant cousin of Maurice and Hanya. He was young, thin and handsome, with light brown hair that kept straying into his bright blue eyes. His smile showed off straight, white teeth and creased a little dimple on one side of his face, and always made the young girls whisper to each other.

"Slawko," Hanya said. "Show some respect."

"To my elders? You mean these two old farts, Ivan and Mike? Sure." He leered at her. "But first, you have to dance with me."

Hanya shook her head, but the pathetic band picked that moment to start a quick waltz. Slawko jumped up, grabbed Hanya by the wrists and spun her onto the dance floor. Hanya cast her brother a look that said "Save me!" But Maurice laughed and Hanya laughed in response, and then waltzed with Slawko across the floor.

It's good to see her laughing, Maurice thought.

"Maurice, Mike never hurt his head," said Ivan, leaning close.

"No?" Maurice put on his best bemused face. "Then how do you account for his memory loss?"

"What memory loss?"

Maurice could not repress his laughter for another second. He punched Mike on the shoulder, tipped his head back and laughed for a long time. It was the first time he had laughed since—he did not want to think how long it had been.

He laughed until tears came from his eyes. Van and Mike stared at him, then looked at each other and back to Maurice.

He brought himself under control as the music ended. The two musicians on the stage announced they were taking a break and Hanya sat down again beside her big brother. Slawko sat on her other side.

"Your sister dances very well, Maurice," he said, panting. He gulped down the dregs of his vodka and choked a little. He smiled at Hanya. Even in the poor light of the hall, his eyes and teeth shone.

Hanya was panting, too, and her face was flushed. "Nonsense," she said. "Slawko is a wonderful dancer." She patted his hand on the table before picking up her own drink.

"More drinks?" asked Slawko. He jumped up and strode to the bar. Hanya's eyes followed him.

"I'll have one!" Mike called after him, but Slawko ignored him.

"What happened to that Luk boy you were seeing?" Maurice asked his sister.

She looked at the floor. "The Germans took him away in September. They rounded up a lot of young men, even some of the bigger teenagers, and put them on a train. They said they were needed in factories in Germany and Poland. His mother got one letter from him. He said he was working on a big farm, heavy labour sixteen hours a day and there was never enough to eat." Hanya sniffed and wiped the back of her hand across her eye. "That was the only time we heard from him. His mother has sent letter after letter back to the return address, but she's heard nothing. Nothing at all."

Hanya looked a the floor for a little longer, then sniffed once more before laughing once and turning a forced smile to her brother. "Enough of that. Tonight is a time to be happy. A new year!"

"Happy new year!" Said Slawko, setting three glasses on the table. He put one in front of Maurice, one in front of Hanya and lifted the third high. Across the table, Mike Babiak scowled at him. "To 1942—may it be a hell of a lot better than 1941!"

"I'll drink to that," Maurice said. He and his sister clinked glasses with Slawko and drank.

"You know, Maurice, I would love to hear more about your experiences in the war," Slawko said.

Maurice drew in a deep breath. He felt his heartbeat accelerate. He looked at Slawko, while the rest of the room, his sister, the Babiak brothers, the party, all seemed to fade away. The clatter, the clamouring, the muted roar of conversations all around faded.

"Why?" he asked.

Slawko shrugged and smiled again. "I'm curious. Where did you go? How many men did you command?"

Maurice's eyes locked on a spot on Slawko's cheek, but he concentrated on the young man's hands. One rested on his knee, the other held his empty glass. The idea that he might throw it flashed into Maurice's mind.

"Kyiv. We started in Kyiv. The Germans pushed us back all the way to Kharkiv."

"Is that where you were taken prisoner?" Slawko asked.

"Where did you hear that?"

Slawko shrugged and smiled even wider. "From people."

Hanya looked at her brother with an expression of puzzlement and alarm.

"How did you escape?" Slawko asked.

Maurice did not answer, but stayed focused on Slawko's hands. He took a chance on a quick look to the front of the hall, but no one new was coming in.

Ivan Babiak piped up again. "Did you kill many Germans, Maurice? Tell us."

Maurice turned to him carefully, but kept Slawko in his peripheral vision. "If I did, Ivash, I am not going to talk about it here."

Ivan slumped in his chair, as sullen as his brother.

"Maurice, relax," said Hanya, putting her hand on his arm. "They're just making conversation."

"Sure, Maurice, it's all right," said Slawko. "If you don't want to talk about it, I understand. So do you, right, Ivan?"

"Sure, Maurice," said Ivan. "Would you like another drink? I would." He frowned at Slawko, who returned a bright smile. "Yes, thanks. Another drink for each of us."

Ivan frowned at Slawko again, but then slapped his brother on the shoulder. "Come help me bring the drinks, Michael."

When her brothers left the table, Maria Babiak leaned closer to Maurice. "I'm sure it must have been terrifying for you in the war."

"It was," Maurice said, nodding.

"Oh, you're so brave!" she said, touching his arm. She looked into his eyes and pushed an errant strand of her black hair over her ear.

God no, not Maria Babiak, he thought.

The band returned to the stage and started playing a polka as the Babiak brothers returned with seven glasses of vodka between them. Slawko was about to ask Hanya for another dance when a tall, slim girl of about 16 ran up and asked him to dance. Slawko agreed with a dazzling smile, which he turned on Hanya as he took the girl to the floor.

"Would you like to dance, Hanya?" Mike Babiak asked.

"Oh, no, I'm still puffed out from the last dance," she lied. "But you go ahead, Maurice."

"No, I don't think—" he began, but Nadia, the prettier of the sisters, ran around the table and took his hand. "Oh, come on, Maurice. Have some fun!"

"No, really, my leg—"

Then Maria was pulling on his other hand. "We're not taking 'no' for an answer, Maurice."

Maurice gave in and let Maria Babiak lead him in a waltz. Then he had to give the next dance to her sister, Nadia, while another of the younger girls commandeered Slawko.

To get away from the Babiaks, Maurice asked for a dance with one of the married women whose husbands had come only to drink. He noticed that Slawko was now dancing with Hanya again.

After a fast polka, Maurice needed a rest. His wounded knee was beginning to ache and his head was sweaty. He could see a blue cloud near the ceiling, so he went near the door and lit a cigarette. Before he shook out the match, he heard a voice say "Here, give me a light, too." It was Slawko Kuritsa.

Maurice held the match while Slawko puffed a cigarette to life. *What does he want? He's not looking for my approval to court Hanya. Is he going to pester me about the army again?*

Slawko spoke so low, Maurice could barely understand him over the music. "You know, I joined Taras Bulba-Borovets' resistance movement," he said.

"Never hear of it," Maurice lied. *He could be a spy.*

"Bulba-Borovets set up the Polissian Sych before the war, but when the Germans arrested the Ukrainian government, he turned against them. Now, we are the Ukrainian Insurgent Army."

"You should stay quiet about things like that, Slawko," Maurice said.

"Why?"

Maurice leaned close and spoke even lower than Slawko. "You don't know who's listening. And you don't know whether you can trust me."

"I know I can trust you. Everyone knows you're a patriot, Maurice."

"Then I'm in real danger."

Slawko put his hand on Maurice's shoulder. "You're among friends, Maurice. Family. Come, join UPA with me. Ukraine needs trained, experienced men like you."

"No. I have had enough fighting. I walked halfway across Ukraine, retreating from the Germans for months, and two more months starving in a prison camp. And you need to learn to keep your mouth shut."

Slawko started to answer, but Maurice's words seemed to sink in. He closed his mouth, shook his head and patted Maurice on the shoulder again before returning to the dance floor.

Maurice did not feel like dancing anymore. He sat down with the Babiaks, lit another cigarette and refused any more requests to dance. He waited until midnight and drank a toast to the new year before telling Hanya he wanted to go home.

"All right, Maurice," she said, disentangling herself from Slawko.

"Going home so early, old man?" he said, beaming his brightest smile at Maurice.

"Good night, cousin. Remember what I told you."

In the buggy, Maurice covered himself and his sister with a thick fur blanket against the cold. He could not imagine being in the field, trying to fight in cold this deep. Is there anyone left alive in the Kharkiv prison camp? Or have the Germans starved them to death by now?

"I don't think you should see Slawko," he told his sister.

"Of course not — he's our cousin, after all," she answered with a little laugh. "We were just dancing. He really is a very good dancer."

"Cousins closer than you and Slawko have married, Hanya. Look at the Babiaks."

"Well, what's wrong with him? He seems quite smart. They say he wanted to go to engineering school before the war started. When things settle down, he might even have the opportunity to study in Germany."

"No Ukrainian is going to study in a university in Germany," Maurice said. "It's not in Germany's plan. But that's not the problem."

"Well, then, what is it?"

Maurice thought about what to tell his sister. "He's reckless. He takes too many chances, not just for his own sake, but people around him, too. Don't tell Mama any of this, but he was talking to me about ..." They were on the frozen road in a moving sleigh, and there was no chance of a German patrol being out on a night like this, let alone close enough to hear them, but he lowered his voice anyway. "...about joining a resistance movement."

Hanya gasped. "Well, that was—how reckless was that? I didn't hear anything. I am sure that he was careful not to let anyone else hear."

"He has no way of knowing for certain that I'm not working for the Germans or the Russians. I was in the Red Army for nearly a year, and after escaping from the POW camp, well, he should be thinking that might mean I had help from the Germans."

"Maurice! No, you could never—"

"You know that, I know it, Mama knows it, some other people, too, but Slawko has no way of being certain. And if he's talking to me about this ... thing, then he's probably talking to other people, too. If he keeps talking, sooner or later some German is going to hear it, or some communist. And when that happens, not only will Slawko be dead, so will everybody he's talked to.

"So stay away from him."

Chapter 3: Recruited

Nastaciv, Ukraine, January 1942

1942 set records for cold. Maurice, his mother and his sister sat next to or on the pietsch, the central oven-cum-furnace, all day to keep warm as icy winds howled around the corners of the house.

Komorski could not hope to keep his pathetic café warm. Ice built up around the windows and at the threshold, where the cold slithered under the door. Like the rest of the patrons, Maurice kept his hat and coat on as they sipped lightly tinted water and exchanged what little news they had. "My poor cows are suffering in this weather," said one, when the door opened and a blast of winter air slapped Maurice's cheek and threw newspapers off the tables. Hrech Zazulak, nearly swallowed by a fur coat and hat, stepped inside and struggled against the wind to pull the door closed again. He shook the snow off himself as he scanned the room. Apparently satisfied with the people he found in the café, he opened his coat and laid it over the back of a chair.

Out of the coat, Zazulak was a tall, thin man with thinning black hair and thick eyebrows. His cheeks were hollow and always covered with black stubble, no matter how recently he had shaved. The day that

Maurice had returned home after nine months of fighting in the Red Army, and weeks starving in a German prison camp, Zazulak had tried to recruit Maurice into a secret underground struggle against the German occupation.

He reached inside the fur coat and took out a broadsheet. "Latest edition, boys." He spread it across the nearest table—*Free Ukraine*, only two days old. "Fritz is taking heavy losses in Tula, and Ivan recaptured Klin to the north weeks ago."

The men gathered around the newspaper, craning their necks to read about German losses across the front, about underdressed soldiers freezing to death. There was a story about a siege of Leningrad, starvation in the streets and cannibalism.

Germany and the USSR had frozen together in a death-grip. "Can you trust this?" Maurice asked Zazulak.

"More than *Pravda* or the shit the Germans spew out," Zazulak said. "But Pravda corroborates the OUN. Read it well, boys, then burn it."

Maurice scanned the rest of the paper as well as he could, sharing it with a half-dozen men. When he looked out the window, he felt a shock at how dark it was. He pulled his scarf up higher on his neck, waved a farewell to Komorski and stepped out, careful to push the door shut.

It opened again and Zazulak stepped out, grabbing for his hat when the wind tore it off his head. He followed Maurice down the road. "You were a member, before the war," he said.

"Don't be ridiculous." Maurice felt his pulse in his neck. "The Communists killed all of OUN in 1939." He sped up, but walking against the wind, in snow half-way to his knees, made for slow going.

Zazulak put his hand on Maurice's shoulder and stopped him. "The Soviets didn't kill all of OUN, and neither have the Germans. And there are other organizations, too. Don't worry, Maurice. I'm not here to betray you."

"It's too cold to stand here. If you want to talk to me, walk with me." Maurice struggled through the snow, head down. The wind stung his face and snowflakes kept landing on his eyelashes.

"Ukraine needs men like you, Maurice," Zazulak said, his voice muffled by his fur coat.

"What do you mean, men like me?" But he knew the answer.

"Men with military experience. Smart men. Able men."

Maurice shivered and pulled his scarf over his nose. He tried to walk faster, but that just made his feet slip back with every step forward.

"Men are building an army for Ukraine," Zazulak continued. "You've heard of the Ukrainian Insurgent Army."

"Never," Maurice lied.

"The Germans dismantled the Polissian Sich," Zazulak said. The Polissian Sich was a military unit commanded by Taras Borovets that defended northwest Ukraine against communist partisans, with the permission of the occupying Germans. But in November 1941, the Germans dismissed the formation and took control of all administrative posts. "Taras Bulba-Borovets has created the Ukrainian Insurgent Army, and he—we want experienced military men like you."

"He calls himself 'Taras Bulba' now?"

If he was smiling, Maurice could not see it for the turned-up collar of Zazulak's coat. "Like the book."

"What's the purpose of the Ukrainian Insurgent Army?

"The goal of UPA is to free Ukraine from the Germans. From all foreigners. To create a free country."

"The Germans don't need our help to destroy Russia. What could a little Ukrainian army do to them?"

"Russia and Germany are going to kill each other. The Red Army has already killed thousands of Germans, and the rest are freezing to death."

"I was in the Red Army. I know how many millions of men died this year, already. So forgive me if I have trouble believing that they can defeat Germany.

"Russia and Germany will destroy each other. Whichever one wins between the two of them will be so weakened they won't be able to withstand a determined, organized revolt. That's Bulba-Borovets' strategy. And until that happens, we need to defend Ukraine against all these occupiers."

"You should not be talking about this to anyone, Zazulak. How do you know I'm not a Communist agent?"

"You a commie?" Zazulak's laughter disappeared into the wind. "You'd sooner sell your mother."

"You do know that I'm a Canadian citizen, right?"

"Canadian?"

"I was born in Montreal. My family moved back here—when we were under Poland—because of the Depression. Would Bulba-Borovets trust me?"

Zazulak shrugged. "I know you were a member of OUN before the war. I know that. So does everyone else, including the Germans, if they care to look it up. You're Ukrainian, and your foreign birth means nothing. It didn't keep you out of the Red Army, did it? Ivan made you an officer."

"That was because of my education."

"Exactly. You're educated, smart, and you have military training. You've seen action. You're what Ukraine needs."

"I fought, Zazulak. I was wounded and nearly lost my leg. I was captured by the Germans and nearly starved to death."

"And then you escaped. You know how important freedom is, Maurice. Help us make Ukraine free."

They had reached the gate in front of Maurice's mother's house. Zazulak stopped. "This war is not over, Maurice. It's barely begun. We thought that Germany was going to liberate us from Stalin, but they just replaced him with Hitler. The Gestapo is liquidating leaders and intellectuals. In the east, in the *Reichskommissariat*, the OUN-M is turning OUN-B members over to the Germans. Even Stepan Bandera will soon have to realize that Russia isn't our only enemy now. Hitler wants Ukraine for Germans. We have to unite to make Ukraine free."

Maurice hesitated with his hand on his mother's gate. He could feel something pulling him toward Zazulak, but the memories of the prison camp in Kharkiv's medieval castle were stronger. The sounds of German guns and bombs, of the dive-bombers in the sky over the Dnipro River filled his mind. He felt again the burning stab of shrapnel in his leg. He looked into Zazulak's eyes, then at his mother's door.

"I don't want to leave my mother alone again," he said.

"Fine. We can use you here."

"For what?"

"Intelligence."

Maurice went to the door of his mother's house. "I'll think about it." As he closed the door, he could see Zazulak walking away, hunched over with his back to the wind.

Chapter 4:
Tekla and the spy
Nastaciv, Ukraine, January 1942

Knocking, insistent yet soft and rapid, woke Maurice. A little greyness leaked around the blind over his window.

Knocking on the door before dawn during wartime — this could not be good.

Maurice padded silently to his door and peeked down the hall. His heart beat fast and sweat beaded his forehead, even though the floorboards sent chills all the way up his legs.

Incredibly, his mother stood at the front door, holding her housecoat closed at her throat with one hand while opening the lock with the other. She opened the door just enough to look outside. "What do you want?" she demanded, and only her children would know from her tone that she was more scared than angry.

"Tesla? Tesla Kuritsa?"

The man was looking for a woman named Tesla.

"Who are you?"

"Andrieski."

"I don't know any Andrieski."

A long silence followed. Maurice crept closer, calculating the moves necessary to get the shotgun from its case if the man at the door tried to force his way in. *Would I be able to get a clear shot without hitting my mother? Mama, get away from the door!*

"What did you say?" Maurice's mother said. Maurice crept a little closer and could hear the man at the door whisper, but he could not make out any words.

"No one is allowed outdoors at this time of the morning," Tekla said. "You had better clear out before you get us both in trouble."

"Are you not Tesla Kuritsa?" the man said. Maurice could hear desperation in his voice.

"No, I am not. Now clear off!"

"It's all right. You can admit it. I am ... a comrade."

Maurice's breath caught in his throat. *A communist— a Soviet agent. He's trying to make contact with Tesla Kuritsa.*

"You're no comrade of mine, mister. I am not Tesla Kuritsa. She is a distant cousin who lives across the river. Now get out before I shoot you myself!" She pushed the door closed and locked it before turning around and leaning on it. Even in the dark, Maurice could see her shaking.

Maurice shook his head to tell her not to speak, then stepped to the front window. He used one finger to move the curtains just enough to see a man walk to the road. He wore warm winter clothing and carried a bag over his shoulder. He looked like any of hundreds of working men, but Maurice knew who he was. *Who he's working for.*

Maurice watched the man until he disappeared down the road, then quickly dressed. He let his mother give him a breakfast of kasha and tea and was out the door by the time the sun turned the sky yellow.

On the doorstep, he turned and embraced his mother. He could feel her shaking in his arms. He realized then this was only the second time he had seen her afraid; the last time was the day he got his draft notice from the Red Army.

That was almost exactly a year ago, he thought. *A day just like today, with snow melting into slush and turning the road to mud.*

He had to walk on the edge of the road, where the ice was a little more solid. He could see the footprints of the visitor in the slush on the way to town, until they turned onto the dirt road that led to the bridge.

Today is going to be different, he promised himself. *I've been between the vise jaws for too long. Ukraine has been in the vise jaws for too long. Germany on one side, Russia on the other, Poland on a third.*

It's time I pushed back.

Maurice continued into Nastasciv and reached Zazulak's house as the sun rose over the snowy fields. Hrech opened the kitchen door after Maurice knocked just once. *Was he waiting for me?*

He nodded at Maurice and let him in, pulling a chair from the kitchen table for him.

Maurice sat. Hrech opened the stove door and stoked the coal before putting a kettle on top. He sat. "We need you to coordinate intelligence reports, code them and deliver them to a drop point."

"That sounds dangerous."

"You will be doing an important task for your country. Ukraine can be free only if we work together."

"That's not why I'm here. Someone knocked on my mother's door an hour ago, looking for Tesla Kuritsa."

"Did you see who it was?"

"No. Just a man. Alone. My mother sent him off and he went across the river."

Hrech drummed his fingers on the table, thinking until the kettle began to whistle. He made two cups of tea without saying anything else until he put the cups on the table. "That means that old communist bastard

Kuritsa is working with the Reds. You know how the Reds operate, don't you?"

"I served in the Red Army for six months."

Hrech nodded. "Good. You'll be perfect for intelligence."

Maurice shook his head. "You have to keep my family safe. No one ever comes to my mother's door in the middle of the night ever again."

Hrech stood again and went to the corner of the kitchen, where he pried a floorboard up. He reached into the space below and brought out a small cloth bag. He carefully replaced the floorboard, and Maurice could not see any sign of it from where he sat.

Hrech took a German-issue pistol, a Luger, from the bag and put it on the table in front of Maurice. "This is for you. You're in UPA, now. I will be your only contact, the only name you know in the army. Everyone else will know you as ..." he looked up, thinking. "Zorenko."

"Little star?"

"Only use it when necessary."

Maurice made himself not look at the pistol. "And my mother?"

"You want her protected? We'll protect her." He pushed the gun toward Maurice. "Make a mask for yourself. Keep it simple. I'll contact you when we need you."

"What about the man who came to my door?"

"We'll take care of him."

"Don't harm Kuritsa!"

Hrech looked Maurice directly in the eyes. "Don't concern yourself with that commie traitor. He's chosen his side, with the Russians. We're fighting for a free Ukraine."

Maurice's mouth was dry. He pushed the guilt away. Kuritsa had chosen a side in this war. Whether Maurice said anything or not, Kuritsa put his own family at risk by offering his home as a contact point for the Soviets.

Maurice stood and slipped the gun into his pocket. He gulped down the rest of his tea and stepped to the door. He had not even taken off his jacket.

"Thank you, Maurice," Hrech said as Maurice opened the door. "You're doing a great service for your country."

Maurice felt the weight of the gun in his jacket all the way back to his mother's house.

He was no longer in the army, he was free of the German POW camp, he was out of uniform, but Maurice's war was far from over.

Chapter 5: The jumper

Nastaciv, January 1942

The next day was not quite as cold. Maurice walked to the village to buy a package of tea and a newspaper. On his way back, Zazulak fell into step beside him. "It's time for your first operation."

Maurice looked over each shoulder, but beyond Zazulak's fur hat, all he saw was snow-covered country houses and two shops. "What are you talking about?"

"The man who knocked on your mother's front door has been all over the village, asking for Teshla Kuritsa."

"Who is he? What does he want?"

"He calls himself Holovchak. He was supposed to get things ready for someone who's parachuting in from Moscow tomorrow night."

"'Things'? What 'things' was he supposed to get ready?"

"He was supposed to meet at Kuritsa's farm with another Russian, a man who parachuted in with a crate of submachine guns. Obviously, the communists have something big planned."

"Where is he now? The man who knocked on the door?"

"In the ground. The boys beat all the information out of him that he had. Now he's no longer a threat to free Ukraine."

Maurice swallowed and looked down the road toward his mother's farm.

"Do you have that gun I gave you?" Zazulak asked.

"It's safe."

"Bring it to Teshla Kuritsa's tomorrow after sunset."

"What about the curfew?"

"The Germans don't dare come out of their armouries after dark. See you then."

As the sun set, Maurice crossed the bridge over the Nishla River and turned toward the farm owned by Ivan Kuritsa, a man distantly related to his mother, Tekla Kuritsa. As if determined to confuse people, he had married a woman named Teshla, a name so similar to Maurice's mother's, Tekla. Newcomers and travelers were always confusing the two.

And now, that confusion has led to a man being beaten to death and has pulled me into a counter-plot, Maurice reflected

Zazulak was already at the gate by the road. In the gloom, Maurice could see four other men. Two held rough wooden clubs, and one carried a Polish-made rifle.

"Ready?" Zazulak asked when Maurice approached. The four men with him nodded, but Maurice stopped.

"Ready for what?"

"Do you have the pistol?" Zazulak demanded, his voice low.

Maurice nodded. The gun's weight at his waist felt reassuring.

"Good. You're going to stand in for Kuritsa. Find out as much as you can from this Commie bastard."

"How do you know he's coming?" Maurice asked.

"We have men watching. Don't worry about that—you don't need to know."

"What about Kuritsa?" Maurice asked.

Zazulak nodded toward the house and the two men with clubs went around the back. The man with the rifle followed Maurice and Zazulak to the front door. Zazulak pounded on it until a rough male voice from behind it demanded "What the hell do you want? It's after curfew. Do you want to bring half the police down on all of us?"

"Open up, Kuritsa. It's Zazulak."

"Go fuck yourself, you fascist prick. Go on, or I'll report you in the morning."

Zazulak put two fingers in his mouth and whistled loudly. Maurice heard banging from inside the house. A woman screamed. Then they heard the male voice shout "What are you doing? Let go of my wife, you bastards!"

Zazulak nodded at the man with the rifle, who rammed the butt into the door. As it burst open, Zazulak rushed inside, Maurice behind him. They chased Kuritsa into the kitchen.

In the kitchen, Kuritsa confronted the two men who gone around to the back door. One held a woman, Teshla, by the shoulders. The other smashed a club into Kuritsa's head.

Kuritsa fell with a howl and Teshla screamed again. "Walter!"

"Sit down, Mrs. Kuritsa. We won't hurt you. Nor your husband, as long as he cooperates and you remain quiet. Pick him up," Zazulak said to the man with the club.

The man grabbed Kuritsa under the arm and shoved him onto a wooden chair. Someone else lit an oil lantern and Maurice could see the small house's interior. It was poor, even by rural standards: a plain birch table, surrounded by hard wooden chairs in varying states of disrepair, stood in front of the stone pietsch, the central hearth-cum-furnace.

Kuritsa himself was a stout, bald man of about forty. He was still wearing his work clothes.

His wife was a short, thin woman with shoulder-length, thin brown hair. The man holding her pushed her gently into another chair, where she trembled and cried quietly.

"Expecting someone tonight, Kuritsa?" Zazulak asked.

"I certainly was not expecting to be attacked in my own home by a bunch of nationalist goons. And you, Bury? What the hell are you doing with a fool like Zazulak?"

"You need not wait any longer. Holovchak is not coming," Zazulak said.

Kuritsa's eyes widened and he opened his mouth, but then closed it without saying anything. He looked at his wife and then said, "I don't know any Holovchak."

"Well, he was certainly asking about you all over the village all day." Zazulak's thick eyebrows came so close together they nearly touched.

"Where is he, then?" Kuritsa was still defiant.

"We took care of him, don't worry."

"What the hell do you want, Zazulak?"

"I want you to tell me all about Kravchenko."

Kuritsa hesitated again. *So he knows the name*, Maurice thought. "Go to hell," Kuritsa said.

"What did Kravchenko want at your little farm, Kuritsa?" Zazulak asked.

"I told you, I don't know any Kravchenko."

"What do you know about a shipment of submachine guns?"

Even in the lamp-light, Maurice could see Kuritsa go pale. He tightened his lips and looked at his wife again, but said nothing.

"Very well." Zazulak motioned to the men with clubs. "Get them out of here. Take Mrs. Kuritsa to my house and keep her comfortable. Take him outside and keep him quiet."

That left Maurice, Zazulak and the man with the Polish rifle in the little farmhouse. "You come with me to the back room," Zazulak ordered. "Bury, when Kravchenko gets here, you tell him you're Kuritsa. Find out where those damned machine guns are."

They waited an hour. Maurice shifted in the hard wooden chair, stood up, paced, sat again. He could hear no sound from Zazulak or the rifleman in the back. He took out his gun, checked the safety and the ammunition, put it away, took it out again, made sure it would slide easily out of the holster. Occasionally he would look out the window, but in the dark night he could not see anything other than a light in the next farmhouse.

Finally he heard a soft knock at the back door. He loosened his pistol again and opened the door a crack. "Who is it?" he asked, voice low. All he could see was the shadowy outline of a man in the dark.

"Tesla Kuritsa?"

Maurice remembered what the first man had said to his mother the day earlier. "Are you ... a friend?"

The shadowy man hesitated. Then he said, "I am looking for Teshla Kuritsa."

"She is my wife," said Maurice. That felt strange.

"I have a message from a mutual friend," said the man.

"Then come in, Comrade," said Maurice, stepping back and opening the door wide.

The shadowed man still waited on the doorstep. "Where is Tesla?"

All Maurice could do was brazen it through. "She could not stay. She is too afraid. But I'm the one you need to talk with, comrade. I've been waiting for you."

"Where is our mutual friend?"

"You tell me." Maurice went to the pietch. "Do you want some tea?"

The man stepped out of the shadows, looking around the kitchen. "I guess so. Did Holovchak contact you?"

Maurice put a kettle on the stove and closed the door. "He came by yesterday before dawn, banging on the door loud enough to wake the dead. He said you would be here tonight, and that's when my wife got scared. But wait—" Maurice held up a hand and looked at the man carefully. He was tall and thin with a slightly hooked nose and a broad chin. He wore a long woolen coat that could have been military issue without insignia, but then, so did almost everyone. "—what's the password?"

The man looked at Maurice as if he could not believe he had asked something so obvious and stupid. *Damn. Was that going too far?*

After a long pause, the man said "Tovarisch. Friend."

Maurice nodded as if in confirmation. "What is your name, Tovarisch?"

The man paused again. "Kravchenko."

The kettle began to whistle. "Aren't you going to make that tea?"

Making tea gave Maurice a chance to calm down. He worried that he would not be able to find the mugs in Kuritsa's cupboard, but his instincts were right and he opened the right door the first time.

Pouring water into cups, a familiar action, made him feel more comfortable. He put a mug on the wooden table and Kravchenko sat. "So, what do you need from me?" he asked.

"What did Holovchak tell you?"

"Nothing." That was true. "Just that you needed my farm."

"You were supposed to have storage ready."

That's interesting. "There's lots of space to store things around here. What do you need?"

"You were supposed to have underground storage ready."

"Yes, yes, comrade, don't worry. What are you storing?"

Kravchenko's eyes narrowed. "Is it ready?"

"Of course, comrade." Maurice sat down opposite Kravchenko and sipped his tea.

"It's not ready, is it? Even after you were specifically instructed."

"We can get this ready very quickly, comrade," Maurice said, waving a hand. "But what is it? If I had an idea what we were storing, we would know what to do."

Kravchenko pushed his chair back from the table. "Who are 'we'?"

Maurice hoped his shock did not show. "There are more than one … of us here." To make up for Kravechenko drawing back, he leaned forward. He could feel the gun's weight on his hip. "What are we getting ready for?"

"You're wasting my time, you fool." Somehow, that statement was worse than the fear and stress Maurice had felt all evening. Kravechenko stood and went for the door.

The UPA man with the rifle stepped in from the back room, rifle leveled at Kravchenko. "Don't move, comrade," he said.

In a single fluid motion, Kravchenko leaned back, kicked the rifleman in the knee and wrenched the rifle from his hands. The rifleman crumpled to the floor.

The variation in weapon design is a curious thing. Most rifles, including the Russian-made Mosin-Sagant, require the shooter to rotate the bolt lever up, then pull it back and push it forward again to load a round into the chamber. The newer rifles that the Polish military began issuing in the 1930s, however, were similar to the

Austrian-made Steyr, which require the shooter to pull the bolt straight back and then forward again, without rotating it around the body of the weapon.

Kravchenko clearly had been trained well. He grabbed the rifle from the Ukrainian guard, turned it in his hands and pulled the bolt lever up.

But the bolt lever on the Polish rifle did not rotate up. Kravechenko pulled it again, eyes fixed on the Ukrainian man rising from the floor.

And then Maurice's Luger was pressed against his temple. "Drop it," Maurice said.

Kravchenko dropped the rifle to the floor and raised his hands. He turned slowly to glare at Maurice, his lips compressed into a thin line.

Zazulak came in with the other man, who still held his club. "Well done, Zorenko." He picked up the rifle and rammed the butt into Kravchenko's chest. The Russian spy grunted and staggered back, but he did not fall and he did not take his eyes from Maurice.

Maurice kept his pistol pointed at him. "What does he want to store at Kuritsa's farm?"

Zazulak turned to the spy for an answer, but Kravchenko's mouth remained shut. "Kuritsa says it's machine guns. Isn't that right, Kravchenko?"

Kravechenko stayed silent.

Zazulak handed the rifle to the man who had brought it. "Take him out of here, but don't let him get the drop on you again."

"Where should I take him?"

"To the cabin. Just keep him quiet. The last thing we need tonight is to rouse Fritz."

The man with the club prodded Kravchenko, who stumbled to the door, the rifleman following. When they were alone in the house, Maurice asked Zazulak "What are you going to do with him?"

"Shoot him, of course. We'll try to get more information out of him, but he's a professional. He won't talk. Not like those fools Holovchak or Kuritsa."

"What are you going to do with them?"

"Holovchak is dead already. We'll execute Kuritsa, too, as a traitor."

"No, don't," Maurice protested, embarrassed to whine.

"Maurice, we have no choice. He knows we're in UPA."

"Everyone in the village knows that already," Maurice said.

"He could tell the Germans."

"Threaten to kill his wife if he does. But don't kill him. He's neutralized as a Soviet agent now—they won't send another agent to him now that Kravchenko and Holovchak have disappeared."

"Maurice, what you're suggesting is very dangerous."

"Please. He's my cousin. Yes, he's distantly related, and he's a fool and a communist and a traitor, but he's family. Don't kill him."

Zazulak shook his head slowly, his eyes full of pity. "Family. I understand, Maurice." He put his hand on Maurice's shoulder. "Family is the basis of our society. It's what we're fighting to protect.

"But what you're asking will put a lot of brave men and women at risk. I'm sorry, my friend. It has to be."

Maurice and Zazulak parted at the bridge, and Maurice walked the rest of the way home alone. He spat onto the side of the road every few steps but he could not get the bitter taste out of his mouth.

Zazulak and his men tortured Kravchenko for days to find out where the machine guns were coming from, but he never made a sound even as his captors broke his bones, knocked out his teeth and burned his feet.

They executed him with a bullet to his brain and threw the body into the river, so that when it was found, it would send a message to the communists that their plan had been foiled.

The Kuritsas, husband and wife, were executed quickly and Zazulak quietly spread the word through the village that UPA would not tolerate traitors.

"And now it's time for you to get busy, Zorenko," he said to Maurice. "Meet me tomorrow."

"What for?"

"You're now in intelligence. Congratulations."

Chapter 6: Intelligence

Nastaciv, January 1942

A week after taking the Soviet spy, Zazulak arrived at Maurice's mother's farm early in the morning. Backlit in the doorway of the barn, huge in his fur coat, he said "Time to start your intelligence work."

Maurice put down the piece of the still he was trying to unblock, put on his coat and boots and followed Zazulak out to the road. "Should I bring the gun?"

"No. The Germans are likely to stop us and search us in the daytime. But keep it with you when you go out after dark."

The trip to Ternopyl took three hours, mostly because Zazulak did not drive there directly. First, he sent the sleigh across fields and stopped at the edge of a forest. He reached from the seat toward a large oak tree as Maurice looked at him, puzzled. Zazulak's hand disappeared into a hollow of the tree that Maurice could not even see, and pulled out a slip of paper. He handed it to Maurice.

"What's this?"

"Intelligence," Zazulak answered, smiling. It was the first time Maurice had seen him smile since returning home. "Open it."

Maurice unfolded the single slip to see strings of Cyrillic lettering that made no sense. "Code?"

"You see? That's why I thought you'd be perfect for intelligence."

"What does it mean?"

"You'll learn the code later."

Zazulak snapped the reins and drove down a narrow path in the forest, stopping at the edge of a clearing. On the other side of it, Maurice could see a disused hunter's shack of weathered gray planks, made for temporary shelter. Zazulak carefully looked around. "No footprints in the snow, so no one has dropped off a message there," he said. "But this is a place you'll check for messages, under the roof at the right-hand corner, there," he pointed. He snapped the reins and they continued. After the forest, they swung into Nastaciv again, stopping at a fence post outside a collapsing abandoned house. Maurice pulled out another coded message from a crack near the top and shoved it in his pocket.

They zigzagged from the edge of one village to the edge of another, stopping at empty structures or innocuous looking spots like the corner of a fence.

As Zazulak had predicted, a German patrol stopped them on the outskirts of Ternopyl, where the road crossed a small bridge. A single soldier stood in the middle of the snow-covered road, pointing a rifle at them. Two others stood on the side of the road. One smoked a cigarette.

Zazulak reined in just short of the soldier in the road, who maintained his aim on the sleigh. The smoking soldier came up to them. His rifle remained slung over his shoulder. "Where are you going?" he asked in German. He sounded bored.

"I don't speak German," Zazulak said to Maurice. "Translate for me." Maurice did, knowing Zazulak was lying. "Tell him we're going to the market in Ternopyl."

"Good morning, sir. We are just going to the market in Ternopyl," said Maurice, smiling at the soldier.

The soldier frowned. "What are you going to buy?"

"Some things for our mother's birthday," Maurice replied. He smiled again. "We're brothers, you see."

The soldier looked at his fellows and frowned again. "You don't look like brothers. Let me see your papers."

"Give him your ID," Maurice told Zazulak in Ukrainian, but Zazulak was already reaching into his pocket, giving Maurice a look that said "Look what you've gotten us into."

Maurice handed both their German-issued ID papers to the soldier. "You're not brothers. You don't even have the same name!"

"We have the same mother, but different fathers," Maurice said, smirking. He leaned closer to the soldier and pointed his thumb over his shoulder. "He's the bastard."

The third soldier burst into laughter. The smoker turned to him to frown, and then back to Maurice and Zazulak. "Get the hell out of here, smart aleck." He thrust the ID papers back to Maurice and waved the solider out of the road.

Zazulak snapped the reins. As the horse passed the checkpoint, he growled "What the hell was that for?" His eyebrows were twin clouds, threatening storm.

"Just a little fun," Maurice answered, chuckling. "In times like these, we need to have some fun once in a while."

"Well, don't do it when we're on a mission again. That kind of fun could get us both arrested and killed."

"On the contrary, Zazulak. It distracted the guards. They were thinking about our promiscuous mother and whether they might sleep with her. They weren't wondering why two farm boys would drive to a city market in the middle of winter without anything to sell."

"Then why did I have to be the bastard?"

"What would you have done in my place?"

Zazulak did not say anything after that, but glared at the road ahead. Maurice settled back and tried to keep from laughing aloud.

They stopped at a two-story tenement near the edge of Ternopyl. Zazulak hitched the horse to a post and led Maurice inside.

The building had a narrow front hallway. On one wall were letter-boxes, one for each apartment. Zazulak took a keychain from his pocket, selected a key and removed it from the chain. "Number 8," he said, and opened the little tin door.

Maurice thought the lock useless. A boy with a screwdriver could have bent the tin easily if he had wanted to steal the mail.

Zazulak took a letter from the mailbox and relocked it, then handed the letter and the key to Maurice. "This is where you'll pick up messages. Only come in here when there is no one else around."

They returned to the sleigh. It was near noon, so Zazulak drove to a small café where they shared a pot of hot tea and a loaf of bread. Maurice was dying to read the letter, but Zazulak put a hand on his arm. "Not here. Not where there is anyone else around."

They finished their meal and got back onto the sleigh. Zazulak set out for Nastaciv again, but Maurice made him stop at a small shop. "What the hell for?"

"We need to buy something for our mother, remember? What else can we tell the soldiers at the check-point?"

They bought two babushkas, the colourful embroidered scarves worn by Ukrainian women. But by this time, the afternoon was getting old and the check-point had moved.

The daylight was failing, but Maurice pulled out the letter. It had no envelope, just a single sheet of paper folded three times and then sealed with a drop of candle wax. The outside was addressed to "Olesh," without address or postage stamp.

He unfolded the letter, but the contents were gibberish—strings of random letters and numbers. "Code?" he asked.

"We call it stefetka," Zazulak answered. "Put it away for now."

They drove to Zazulak's house, attached to his little machine shop. Zazulak poured Maurice a glass of vodka and set the oil lamp to its brightest, then taught Maurice the code. It seemed complex at first, but once Maurice understood its underlying logic, he could soon understand the messages immediately upon reading them, without deciphering them.

The first message comprised two fragments.

6 wehrmacht infantry units moving east for Ternopyl.
Panzers on trains headed for Kyiv.

Maurice knew that already: he had seen the trains, packed with soldiers, flatcars bearing tanks and self-propelled field guns, leaving Ternopyl for the eastern front.

"What can we do with this information?"

"Coordinated with information from all over Ukraine, it can be priceless," said Zazulak. "You are now responsible for intelligence reports from the countryside around Ternopyl, from Tereblovya to Zbaraz, Taurov to the Proskurov oblast," Zazulak said, describing an area around the city about 70 kilometres across. "You'll decode them, compile them and code messages to leave at the apartment in Ternopyl."

"Where do they go from there?" Maurice asked, even though he knew better.

"Taras Bulba-Borovets," the leader of Ukrainian resistance in the German-occupied lands, whose nickname came from Nikolai Gogol's novel about seventeenth-century Cossacks. "Your code name is 'Zorenko,'" meaning "star."

"Your contact from now on is Volovets," a code name that was a play on the Ukrainian word for "pencil." "Your job is to pass on important information. Leave out the bullshit."

Over the next week, Zazulak took Maurice to the places where UPA observers dropped off their messages: hollows in fence-posts, between two boards on a farm shed, in a hollow tree off the road. After the snow melted in the spring, agents could hide the messages in the forests, under rocks or in a narrow crotch between branches. The paper might be stained, torn and crumpled, but the information was precious.

Germans take 20 boys from Lviv, sent west through Polissia.

Two German infantry units transferred from Vilnius east on Kharkiv line.

The Germans kept Ternopyl's and Lviv's train stations busy all the time, because they were two of "break of gauge" points. The rail gauge in most of Europe was 4 feet, 8 1/2 inches. However, at the end of the 19th century, Tsar Nicolas II had declared that Russian trains would use a wider gauge of five feet. This small difference meant that European rail cars could not travel on Russian railways and vice-versa. It also meant that at the "break of gauge" points, near the old borders of the Russian Empire, goods and people had to get off one train and onto another to continue their journeys.

This activity kept stations in Brest, Belarus, and in Lviv—called Lwow when it was part of Poland—and Ternopyl, also known as Tarnopol under the Poles and Russians, busier than stations in similar-sized cities in other countries in Europe. Ternopyl was also busy as a crossing of the line from Odessa to the Polish border and the north-south line.

But train movements were not the only information that the hidden UPA agents sent.

Polish partisans attacked German armoury in Ozernyany.

Soviet-communist partisan unit from Polissia moved to Halychyna and attacked UPA unit south of Synava. UPA killed 6, drove them north. Lost 2 men: B. Demchyshyn L. Kozachenko

Some messages twisted Maurice's guts.
Ukrainian and Polish partisans fighting in Halychyna. Losses on both sides.

OUN (B) attack Polish village in Volhynia. 12 civilians killed.

The most desperate messages told of the German crackdown on Ukraine.

Gestapo arrested mayor and council office of Taurov, sent them west.

SS unit surrounded four Jewish villages in Volhynia, killed or deported all inhabitants.

Another message corroborated this one.

Cattle cars packed with civilians, probably Jews, heading east. Transferred to Polish rail at Lviv.

Occasionally, he would find a message from his commander, Volovets, in the mailbox in Ternopyl.

OUN (B) encouraging Ukrainian men to join German-organized police force for training. Not Zorenko. Let others join.

Maurice got information, also, from more sources than these terse notes from unknown men in the forests and villages. Bulba-Borovets' sporadic newspaper, *Haidamaka*, brought increasingly alarming news: Stepan Bandera, head of the Ukrainian government-in-exile, in prison in Germany, called for ethnic cleansing of Poles and Jews from Ukraine. Bulba-Borovets opposed the idea. "Ukraine has more significant enemies than Poles and Jews," he wrote.

There were stories from the brutal Nazi occupation of the bulk of Ukraine, the *Reichskommissariat* administered by Erich Koch. He called himself a "brutal dog" and said his job was to "suck from Ukraine all the goods we can get hold of." He also instructed his subordinates to use "the utmost severity towards the native population."

Messages came through other channels, as well, passed from person to person, somehow filtering back from the east. These messages described the Germans gathering Jews, civic leaders and Ukrainian nationalists as well as communists in Kyiv, shooting them by the hundreds and thousands and dumping the bodies in a ravine called Babyn Yar. "In one day last September," one man whispered in Komorski's cafe while the locals leaned close so they would not miss a single word, "the Germans, they call them the Einsatzgruppen, the death squads, they killed over thirty thousand Jews. Hundreds of Ukrainians, too. There's not a communist or even a socialist left alive in Kyiv."

The rural winter of 1942, the winter that stopped the German advance into Russia, ended with melting snow and overflowing streams in April. The Nazi empire was at its peak. Hitler and his henchmen ruled Europe from the Atlantic coast to the Don River and the Russian steppes, from north of the Arctic Circle to the Mediterranean. The Italians held Libya and the Germans controlled Algeria through their puppets in Vichy France. Hitler's administrators were bending the entire economy of Europe to feeding the Nazi war machine, a beast that would inevitably consume itself.

The warm weather finally freed Europe from winter's icy grip, but that also freed the Germans from the disadvantage they had in the winter. Through the spring, they reversed the Soviet advances made in the winter and began a drive toward the Caucasus oil fields and the city of Stalingrad, at the great bend of the Volga River.

In Ukraine, they began implementing a new policy.

Germans confiscating food from farms. All units to stop them, seize food from German stores, return to the people.

The Germans had maintained the collective farm system Stalin had imposed on Ukraine. But the Germans confiscated all the harvests to feed their armies. They also confiscated harvests from smaller farms, leaving scraps for the farmers, and sent thousands of young men and women west to be slaves.

Maurice began planning an operation, but it would wait for warmer weather.

Chapter 7: Re-routing trains

April 1942

Maurice knew who was knocking at the first rap. It was after curfew.

"Zazulak," he said before he fully opened the door.

"Are you ready to go?" Zazulak asked. He wore dark clothing. In the moonlight, Maurice could just see a thin belt across his chest, and on his hip, a holstered pistol.

"Ready to go where?" Maurice asked, but he knew.

From the corner of his eye, he could see his mother in the hall, her hand in front of her throat.

Zazulak thrust a bundle of cloth into Maurice's hands. He turned and walked down the front steps without looking to see whether Maurice followed. "Ready to get off your ass and serve your country."

The bundle was heavier than it looked. Maurice pulled back the top fold to see two leather belts and a holster.

"I don't have all night," Zazulak called over his shoulder. "You can put that on later. I'm just tired of carrying it."

Maurice tucked the bundle under his arm and hurried back to his room. He fetched the Luger Zazulak had given him from its hiding place, shoved it into the empty holster and wrapped the cloth—he could see now that it was a pair of pants, a shirt and a jacket—around the belts again.

He paused at the door. "I'll be all right. Don't worry that I won't be back before midnight. Don't open the door for anyone until I get back home," he said to his mother, who stood by the pietsch, her hand at her throat. He grabbed a hat, his warm jacket and boots and ran after Zazulak, who was walking down the road toward the village.

The night was chilly, a reminder of the brutal winter that was only reluctantly letting go of eastern Europe. Snow, dirty and crusty, still remained under the trees and in deep ditches. Maurice wished he had thought about bringing gloves as well, but it was too late to go back.

"Where are we going?" he asked when he caught up with Zazulak.

"You'll find out when we get there. Now shut up."

Maurice stopped and waited for the other man to notice. "Zazulak, if you want my help, you'll tell me what it's for. Or I'll just go back home."

The mechanic opened his mouth but no words came out. Maurice watched him struggle to find the words. Finally, he stepped closer and whispered: "We have something to do, but I'm not going to discuss it out here. You obey me—"

"No. I'm the officer here, remember? You're just a mechanic with a gun. I'm the military man. I said, if you want my help, you tell me what for. Even the Red Army told its soldiers where they were going." *Usually*, he added to himself.

Zazulak stood fidgeting. He could not decide how much to tell this troublesome new recruit to the cause. "It's not safe to talk here, Maurice. We're going to meet some others, and then we're going to…" He leaned even closer and whispered in Maurice's ear: "The train yards."

Maurice nodded. *This is serious*, he thought. "All right. Let's go."

They continued without another word. Soon after they crossed the bridge over the river, Zazulak stepped off the road onto a track through the trees. Maurice had known that path since he had been a boy. He remembered playing there and knew it led to a rocky clearing and a small bluff where young people would come on warm summer nights to make love.

Zazulak stopped before he stepped into the clearing. In the moonlight, Maurice could barely see him.

"Put it on before we meet the others," he said.

"The uniform? What if the Germans catch us?"

Zazulak laughed. "If they catch us outside after curfew, they'll shoot us no matter what we wore. But there are no Germans out after dark, Maurice. UPA rules the night."

Maurice handed his jacket to Zazulak and shrugged on the black uniform of the Ukrainian Insurgent Army. Zazulak tried to help pull it straight, but Maurice shrugged him off, annoyed. It may have been a different colour, but otherwise it was identical to the jacket he had worn as a lieutenant in the Red Army. He didn't need anyone's help to put on a uniform.

Dressed and buckled, he followed Zazulak into the clearing, who stepped out of the trees and stopped again. "*Rosy chervy*," he said, Ukrainian for "dew worms."

"Plenty tonight," said a voice from the clearing.

Zazulak stepped ahead as the moon rose above the trees. Maurice could just make out six men in the same dark uniform he wore. *Dew worms. If a German patrol heard us, we could say we're collecting bait for fishing.*

Except that it's not fishing season. And we're wearing insurgent uniforms.

His heart pounded. Every sound seemed amplified into a riot of rustling leaves, crunching sticks. Even the whisper of his pant legs sounded loud enough to draw a German patrol from a mile away.

"This is Zorenko," said Zazulak, indicating Maurice. "He joined us in the winter."

One man stepped closer, just a mix of shadows in the gloom under the moon. Maurice recognized Evhen Mackiw, the baker's son. Mackiw looked him up and down. "Does he know how to use a gun?"

"Better than you," Zazulak said, laughing. Mackiw did not look amused. "He has a Luger."

"Shouldn't we check him out before letting him have a gun?" Mackiw said, but Zazulak cut him off.

"I'm in charge of this unit. If I say give him a gun, he gets a gun."

"But—" Mackiw began, and Zazulak lashed out, a fist straight to the baker's son's nose. Mackliw went down on his butt, and one of the other men in the shadow behind him laughed.

"Shut up," Zazulak ordered. "Check your weapons. The night's getting old."

Maurice checked the safety on his Luger, made sure the chamber was empty, and then checked the magazine, which fit in the handle. Although he had never fired one before, he had learned how to use the German automatic handgun during officer training. "What are we doing tonight?" he asked again.

"We are going to cause some problems for Fritz's supply lines," said one of the men in the clearing.

How did they avoid the draft, Maurice wondered. *Was I the only unlucky one, or did they escape somehow?*

"Shut the fuck up, I said," Zazulak ordered. "No more talking until we get to the target. Just follow me. Only because you'll burst if I don't tell you, Zorenko, the target is the train station. We'll stay off the roads. Stay away from light and walk carefully. No noise. If

Fritz finds us before we get there, I'll myself shoot whoever made noise!"

Zazulak led them down another path beneath the trees until they reached a man with a horse-drawn carriage, waiting in a clearing. "Rosy chervy," Zazulak said again, softly.

"Plenty tonight," the man said. Maurice thought the voice sounded familiar. Oleskiw, the carpenter, he remembered. They all climbed into the back. Oleskiw snapped the reins, the noise making Maurice flinch, and they set off along narrow paths, skirting the edges of farms.

The only sounds were the horse's hoof-falls on soft earth and the creaking of the wheels and body of the wagon. The moon sank below the trees, and an hour and a half later, they emerged from the forest at a high barbed-wire fence. "Careful, boys," Zazulak hissed as they climbed down from the wagon. Oleskiw led the horse and wagon back into the forest to hide them.

Zazulak led the group between the fence and the tree line, to a spot where a bush seemed to reach for the fence. He pulled the branches away and Maurice realized that they had disguised a spot where the fence wires had been cut. Zazulak pulled the wires to one side and the men of the party slipped inside, one by one. "Look around," he whispered. "Memorize this spot. If things go to shit, it's the only escape."

Inside the fence, Maurice realized they were in the train yards south of Ternopyl. Silhouetted by lights on the station and other buildings, lines of boxcars stood on ranked rails like sleeping cattle.

Zazulak held one finger over his lips and gestured the other forward. Maurice copied his crouching run to the end of a series of boxcars and then around it.

Zazulak halted deep in the shadow between two trains. He pointed at one of the cars. Oleskiw jumped onto the ladder built onto its side and Maurice cringed at the soft ring of his boots on the rungs. At the top, Oleskiw pulled a large white card from a frame on the side of the car and clambered back down.

Another man climbed the ladder of the car on the train beside the first one, brought down the card and exchanged for the one in Oleskiw's hand. Then the two men re-climbed the ladders and replaced the cards.

"What the hell are they doing?" Maurice whispered.

"Switching the destination cards," Zazulak explained. "Those cards indicate where each car is supposed to go. At each switching station—like this one—the Germans use the cards to tell where to send the car and how to organize the trains. Now, they'll get the wrong supplies at different destinations along the front."

"So? What good does that do?" Maurice whispered as he watched Mackiw and Oleskiw repeat their card exchange at the next pair of boxcars. "The supplies still get to the front."

"You were an officer on the front lines, Maurice," Zazulak said. "Think about what it would mean if you got extra socks when you needed ammunition."

"We never got extra socks and we were always short of ammunition."

"Shut up." Zazulak turned to the other men. "What you're doing is good, but it's not efficient. Here's what we're going to do. We form two teams of four. Two climb the ladders and throw down the cards to a man on the bottom. The men at the bottom run across and exchange the cards, then bring them back to the man on the ladder. The men on the ladders replace the cards, while the ground men go to the next car and climb the ladders. Switch roles, repeat to the end. Then it's back to the hole in the fence. Zorenko, you're with me."

Zazulak ran around the end of the train, sprinted across a patch lit by a lantern at the end of the station house, and dashed between the last two trains next to the station. Maurice followed, heart hammering as he crossed the lit patch. He expected an alarm, followed by a bullet in his chest, but the train yard remained quiet. He could see Zazulak scrambling up a ladder. He dropped the card and Maurice caught it, surprised at its weight and stiffness. It's wooden, he realized. Not cardboard. Of course; cardboard would dissolve in the rain.

"Go!" Zazulak hissed. Maurice ran across the space between the trains and traded the wooden card with Mackiw. Then he ran back to where Zazulak hung from the ladder's lowest rung, hand outstretched.

Zazulak grabbed the card and climbed up. Maurice ran to the next car. He had to jump to get his foot on the bottom rung, and he banged his knee on the next.

How does the card come out? He had to press his hand flat against the surface and push the wooden card up and toward him. He nearly overbalanced, banging his shoulder on the ladder as he caught himself.

Finally, he could grasp the edge of the sign beyond the frame that held it. He pulled it out and started down the ladder again.

"Hurry up!" Zazulak said as he took the sign. Maurice clung to the ladder, arm shaking, until Zazulak returned with the other card. Marice took it, but his hand was slippery with sweat and he dropped it. It clanged on the ground and Zazulak swore. He picked it up and held it until Maurice had a firm grip. "Be quick, Zorenko," he whispered, then ran to the next car.

As fast as he dared, Maurice climbed back up, shoulder aching where he had banged it. The sign slid easily into its frame and Maurice climbed back down, worrying about the noise every time his boots touched a metal rung.

Zazulak was already waiting with a sign at the bottom of the next ladder. Maurice ran, grabbed it, exchanged it with Mackiw, gave the new sign to Zazulak and ran to climb the next ladder.

In this way, they worked along the trains, moving always closer to the station-house. There were three cars left when they heard a bark.

They all froze, looking at each other. The dog barked again.

Zazulak nodded and all four men ran as fast as they could to the end of the train and turned toward the far end of the yard. As he passed the next train, Zazulak slapped the side of the last boxcar as a signal to the other team.

The dog started barking incessantly. Another dog joined the chorus, farther away but coming closer.

Their only sounds were panting breath and pounding feet, the eight men scrambled to the hole in the fence. Zazulak held the strands apart until the others squeezed through, and then followed. He threw the branch back over the hold and threw himself under the trees. Maurice threw himself flat on the ground beside him, just as he heard the dogs reach the fence, growling. He dared to raise his head just enough to see under the branches. Two German Shepherds sniffed at the edge of the fence, growling, moving their heads back and forth as they searched for the men.

Behind them, Maurice saw lanterns approaching. He prayed the other men on his team knew enough to stay still and quiet.

As the lamps came closer, they threw enough light for Maurice to see one dog sniffing, dashing back and forth as if it sensed the men hiding in the bushes on the other side. The other stood back a few metres from the fence, growling continuously and looking from side to side.

"Ho, boys, what is it? What do you see?" a guard carrying a lantern said in Ukrainian. He reached the second dog. It turned to him and whined, then pointed its nose directly to the spot where the wire fence had been cut.

Another guard came up, holding his lantern high to cast light as far as possible. "What is it?"

"I don't know. I don't see anything."

"Were they chasing rabbits again?"

"Naw. Voke never gets this excited over rabbits. Look at him—he's practically tearing the fence down."

The two guards stepped close to the fence, lifting their lanterns high and squinting for any sign of whatever might have set off their dogs. Voke sniffed along the fence until it was directly in front of Maurice. To his horror, it raised its head and looked him directly in the eye. It growled.

Maurice pushed himself back, keeping his belly flat on the wet ground and the dog barked once more.

Maurice froze and cold mud oozed into his boots.

"What is it, Voke?" said the first guard, running over and lifting his lantern high again. The dog started barking continually. It jumped at the fence and fell back, whining.

Maurice scrambled backwards until the bushes allowed him to turn around. He ran in a crouch, crashing through the brush until he stumbled onto a path. Around him, he could hear his comrades doing the same.

"There's someone there, all right!" one of the guards yelled. "A whole bunch of them! Good dogs!"

"Should we go after them?" the second guard asked.

"Not by ourselves. And by the time we get some fellows to come with us, they'll be long gone."

"They must have come through the fence somewhere near here. Plus, we have dogs! We can track them."

"Look, I'm not going out there at night. Those woods are full of UPA partisans. Second, who do you think the Germans will blame if they found out how saboteurs got into the yard?"

"What do you think they wanted?"

"Let's check the trains for open cars and bombs. Other than that, let Fritz worry about Fritz."

Maurice and the rest pounded down the trail until they could not run anymore. They halted, puffing, at the clearing where their horse and wagon waited. As their breathing slowed, Zazulak asked "Is everyone here?" He counted them, ending by touching his chest. "Eight. Good. Is everyone all right?"

"I tore my uniform," one said.

"We're all fine," said Maurice.

"Good. Now, back home," Zazulak ordered. "Not a word about this operation to anyone. Hide your uniforms. We'll reconvene here in a week."

They mounted the wagon, Oleskiw at the reins again, and rode in silence. When they arrived at their starting point, the boys disappeared into the night, until only Maurice and Zazulak were left. They began walking back to Nastisiv.

"So that's what we do? Play with the trains?" Maurice asked. "It may inconvenience Fritz, but surely we can do some more effective things."

"Those are the orders for now," Zazulak answered. "Disrupt, confuse, harry. Help Ivan to wear Fritz down until they're both crippled.

"I have some doubts about that," said Maurice.

Maurice had no way of knowing that, only a few months later when the Germans reached Stalingrad on the Volga River, missions like this would have a huge impact. With their supply lines stretching along vulnerable railways across thousands of miles of enemy territory, the Germans needed to control the movement of every uniform, every medical kit, every round of ammunition. And toward the end of the Battle of Stalingrad, which still ranks as the bloodiest, deadliest in the history of warfare, the battle that proved Germany's defeat was inevitable, the desperate invaders would open boxcars labelled "ammunition," to find crates of prophylactics.

Chapter 8:
Slawko Kuritsa

Nastaciv, Ukraine, April 1942

Maurice arrived at the market in Nastaciv to find the village buzzing. It was the first warm day of the spring, and the sunshine seemed to put the villagers of Nastaciv into a cheerful mood.

"They attacked the armoury last night," people kept saying as they set up their stalls or picked over onions and carrots.

"Who did?" Maurice asked as he started to unload crates of new beets.

People would lean closer and whisper harshly: "UPA, of course. Brazen!"

"Fearless," said someone else.

"No good will come of this. The Germans won't let this go," said a third.

"Six German soldiers killed, the building destroyed and the insurgents got away with wagon-loads of guns, bombs and ammunition," said a young blond man who could not help looking pleased.

Why didn't I know about this? Maurice wondered. But he could not say that aloud.

The Germans did not take long to respond. Before noon, a staff car with red and black swastika flags flapping roared into the square, followed by a truck, its back covered with cloth. They screeched to a halt in the middle of the square and soldiers holding submachine guns jumped down. Two reached into the back of the truck and pulled out men wearing civilian clothes. Their hands were tied together and most fell as they got out of the truck. The soldiers kicked them and hit them with the butts of their rifles until they stood in a rough line.

Maurice recognized young men, all from Nastaciv or farms close by. His breath caught when he saw a young man with tousled brown hair and bright blue eyes: Slawko Kuritsa, his cousin who had danced with his sister on New Year's Eve.

The soldiers shoved their prisoners toward the centre of the square as a young officer got out of the staff car. Very erect, his uniform perfectly cleaned and pressed to razor sharpness, he strode, erect and calm, toward the prisoners.

The market was silent. The April breeze stopped, and the villagers stood, riveted in the bright sunshine.

"Are these the suspects from last night's attack?" the officer asked in German, in a clear voice that everyone in the market could hear.

"Yes, Hauptman!" a sergeant responded.

The captain walked up and down the line of bound men, looking at each one critically. "Which one of you is the leader?" he demanded, walked to the end of the line, turned and walked back. "Which one gave the orders?" he repeated.

No one answered. The captain walked back down the line, peering at each prisoner. No one else made a sound. The entire market was riveted by the display.

"Tell me which of you is in charge. He will be punished. The rest of you will go free, on my honour as a German officer."

Still no one spoke. The prisoners looked at the ground, knowing what was about to happen.

Someone in the crowd spoke up. "They're only boys, for God's sake. Let the youngest ones go." Maurice turned to see who it was: an older woman with a kerchief on her head—Anna Kovalchuk, who lived alone. Her husband and son had been killed when the Germans swept through Ukraine.

The officer nodded once, and a soldier stepped up to Anna and clubbed her head with his rifle butt. She fell without making a sound, and the rest of the crowd gasped as one.

The officer turned to face the crowd. "These men attacked the German army last night, a cowardly ambush on the armoury. They killed six of my men, betraying the Nazi party that liberated your country from communism. We cannot and will not tolerate this treason.

"One more time," he said to the prisoners. "Which of you is in charge? Give him up, and the rest will go free." He waited for several seconds, but the prisoners only looked at the ground. "Very well," he said. He walked to one end of the line and started counting off the prisoners. "*Ein, zwei, drei...*"

Maurice felt sick to his stomach. *No, don't let him do it,* he thought. When the officer reached ten, he was standing in front of Slawko. Calmly, the officer drew his Luger sidearm from its shiny leather holster. Maurice could see Slawko shaking. His own hands shook, too. The officer pressed the barrel of his pistol against Slawko's head and squeezed the trigger.

A pathetic pop echoed across the square. Slawko's body dropped like empty rags. A woman cried out. Men moaned, and Maurice realized he was one of them. He felt his tears on his cheeks.

"Put the rest in the lockup," the officer said. "Tie the body to a post in the square. Let it be a reminder to the people about what happens to traitors to the Third Reich."

Slawko's body remained tied to a post with barbed wire, with a sign around its neck that read "This is what happens to traitors to the Third Reich." Finally, one night, someone cut the decomposing body down and his family held a secret service in the forest to bury him.

Chapter 9: Night raid

Seredynky, Ukraine, July 1942

Sitting on a wagon, the smell of horse and pine in his nostrils, Maurice did a quick count: eight volunteers, plus himself. Four experienced UPA fighters, men armed with rifles and sidearms, dressed in the black uniforms of the insurgent army. They had another four-wheeled wagon drawn by two horses.

The rest were earnest locals in civilian clothing. Roman was either very short for his age, or no more than fourteen years old. Maurice had been unwilling to accept him as a volunteer until he said he could bring a horse and cart from his farm. The other teenager, Leon was a tall lad with black hair sticking out from under his cap. A beautiful young woman stood next to Leon, wearing a man's cloth cap crammed onto her long blond hair and a determined expression. The only things Maurice knew about her were that she was named Yulia, she came from Yospivka, another tiny village west of Nastaciv, and her father had been taken away by the Germans.

Only one of the four, a middle-aged tailor, had an old shotgun. The rest were weaponless.

It would have to do.

Maurice glanced up. The last yellow glow of the sun was about to die behind the trees, but the air was still hot and sticky. He surveyed his little band again and gestured them to gather closer in the middle of the little clearing in the forest. He kept his voice low, even though he knew the chances of a German patrol, or anyone else for that matter, being this deep in the woods after dark were almost nonexistent.

"The Germans have been confiscating food from farms across Volhynia and Halychyna. You all know this."

"They've taken everything my family has grown this year," said Roman, the boy on the cart. "The family on the farm next to ours is starving, and they have a small baby."

"They took my daughter," said the tailor. He was a small, thin but wiry man with deep wrinkles next to his eyes. He walked with a pronounced limp. "She's fifteen. I don't know where she is. I only know she's either dead or a whore now."

Maurice nodded. "Tonight, UPA is striking at storage locations across the region, all at the same time. Our objective is a barn storing grain outside Seredynky," a village four kilometres north of Nastaciv. "It will be guarded. We will have to kill the guards and take what we can on these wagons."

"Is it going to be dangerous?" asked Leon, the taller boy. One of the UPA men laughed, a short bark that was too loud for Maurice's liking. He glared at the man and then turned to the boy.

"Very dangerous. That's why silence is essential," Maurice answered. "You all know the way to Seredynky. We'll each take a different path and meet under the trees, east of where the railroad crosses the river, in an hour. No talking until then, and when you see anyone else from the group, give them this sign." He held up three fingers, then closed his fist and held up his thumb. "Got that?" The group nodded.

He nodded at the UPA men. Kushnir, a sharp-faced man Maurice's age, climbed in beside him. Marchuk, who had a broad scar across his face, climbed into Leon's wagon with Serhiy, the tailor. A third soldier whom Maurice knew only as "Hammer" held the reins of the third wagon. Hammer had been the man who had hit Kuritsa with a club that night in January. He was a short man with broad shoulders and a barrel chest. Beside him was the fourth UPA man, a tall, lanky man code-named Shyp, or "Spike."

Yulia climbed into the back of Maurice's wagon. Maurice turned around to see that she was settled on the bed of the wagon. She looked at him and nodded, but even in the moonlight, he could see the fear in her eyes.

Maurice slapped the reins and directed the horse along a narrow path under the trees. Hammer's wagon squeaked and groaned as he found another path along a stream.

The sound of another horse clopping behind him made Maurice turn again. Leon followed him. Maurice shook his head and pointed toward a third path, the least direct route to the village of Seredynky, but the safest. The boy pulled the reins and looked frightened, but Marchuk poked his shoulder and pointed in the same direction. The boy complied. Maurice reined in and watched until the wagon disappeared into the gloom beneath the trees.

He started again. It would take his wagon almost an hour to get to Seredynky along the quickest, most direct route. He glanced at the rifle between Kuchnir's knees and the Luger in the holster at his own hip. He rehearsed the plan in his mind: converge under the cover of trees near the little bridge where the railroad crossed a little creek to the east of the village. From there, they would dismount and creep close to the barn where the Germans stored food they had confiscated from local farmers. At exactly midnight, coordinated with strikes by other UPA groups across the Ternopyl region, they'd take out the guards as quietly as possible, break open the barn and load as much as they could onto the wagons, then disappear as quickly as they could to UPA hideouts in the forests.

It sounded simple, but Maurice knew how dangerous it was. He was glad there were experienced guerrillas in the group with him, but feared for the young boys and the woman behind him.

The moon set before Maurice reached the railway track. The night was as dark as Maurice had ever seen, with only starlight overhead. He reined in and patted the horse's hindquarters as it snorted. Silence was essential. He motioned to Kuchnir and Yulia, and they climbed off the wagon as quietly as they could.

A few minutes later, repetitive squeaking announced the arrival of Hammer and Spike in their wagon. They all made the hand signal Maurice had shown. Maurice ground his teeth until the wagon stopped and the noise of the two men and the tall teenager climbing down and taking their weapons ceased. He let out a breath when the only sounds he could hear were crickets and the gentle lapping of the water in the stream.

Now, they only had to wait for the third wagon, the one driven by Leon, which he had sent by the safest but longest route. Maurice began to feel anxious. *What if they were arrested, caught by the Germans despite the precautions we took?* he thought. He squinted at his watch, struggling to see the time in the dark. *Getting close to midnight.*

Boys that young shouldn't have to fight in a war, he thought. But he knew that neither he, the UPA nor the boys themselves had any choice. All he could do would be to try to give them the lowest-risk assignments.

Maurice let a breath out when, at five minutes to midnight, he heard the soft clopping of a horse's hooves and the squeaking of a wagon. The last wagon emerged from the shadows under the trees, and in the starlight, Maurice could make out Marchuk sitting beside the boy with the reins in his hands. The boy made the hand signal as he reined in.

"All right," Maurice said in a soft voice, "Hammer, Spike, Marchuk, Kuchnir, you come with me. I'll cut the fence. You—" he pointed at Leon on his wagon "and you"—he pointed at Roman "and you"—at Yulia "will bring the wagons across the railway tracks and wait under the trees until you get the signal. Then bring the wagons to that barn." He pointed across the tracks, where an old barn stood surrounded by a chain-link fence. "Load as much as you can as fast as you can, then get out and back the same way you came. Any questions?"

"What do you want me to do?" asked the tailor.

"Watch for the Germans." Maurice pointed beyond the barn to another building, an old shop about a hundred metres away. "That's the garrison. If you see anyone coming, whistle. Kill as many as you can, and get out fast."

Maurice nodded at the UPA men. They readied their weapons and walked, crouching low and trying not to make any noise, quickly over the train tracks. At the fence, Maurice pulled wire cutters out of his pocket. He cut the links upwards, then across to make an opening large enough for a horse and wagon, glancing up toward the barn and the garrison building beyond it every time the cutters made a snip noise. Marchuk and Hammer pulled the fence back, bending the wires so it would stay open.

When the opening was large enough to bring a horse and wagon through, Maurice looked carefully at the barn. He could see one guard at the door, and knew there would be one more on the other side.

Maurice nodded at Hammer. He and Marchuk crept inside the fence, crossing the three metres to the barn noiselessly. Taking a long knife from a sheath at his hip, Hammer came up behind the guard, stood quickly and slashed the guard's neck. He fell without a sound into Hammer's arms, who laid the body on the ground gently and relieved it of the rifle.

Marchuk disappeared around the barn as Maurice and the remaining two UPA men entered the fence. Maurice heard a gurgle and a clatter as Marchuk dispatched the other guard.

Maurice looked toward the garrison again, but saw only the tailor, who had made his way around the outside of the fence and stood facing the farther building. Maurice turned to the door of the barn. No lock? "Give the signal for the wagons," he said. Spike waved his hands toward the opening in the fence.

One of the horses snorted and neighed once at the opening, but the young boy was leading it by the bridle and pulled its head down so it could get through. Maurice nodded at Hammer, who opened the barn door.

A blast knocked Hammer into Marchuk behind him, and Maurice could not move for long seconds as he accepted the presence of another guard inside the barn, holding a smoking rifle. The guard drew back the bolt for another shot, but Spike and Kuchnir fired their rifles at the same moment, and the guard fell.

Maurice swore, kneeling beside Hammer. Dead. "Put him in the wagon," he said to Kuchnir.

The first wagon was beside the door, its horse moving nervously, trying to push its way back. The young boy driving it no longer held the bridle, but stood still, eyes wide. "Quiet that horse," Maurice ordered. "Load as many bags and barrels as you can. Hurry."

Kuchnir and Marchuk pulled Hammer's body into the back of the wagon. Maurice and Spike loaded sacks of flour beside him. "Go on, get that out of here and make room for the next wagon."

The boy led the horse around the barn, back to the opening in the fence as the other teenager led the next wagon over. Everyone pitched in, loading barrels and sacks. Minutes felt like hours, like days as Maurice kept looking toward the garrison. Sweat stung his eyes and made his shirt cling to his skin.

With the second wagon full, Maurice slapped the horse's rump, sending it around the barn like the first. Yulia led the third wagon, and the men had only loaded one sack onto the back when they heard the tailor's voice. "Get out! Fritz is coming."

Maurice looked up as the tailor melted into the shadows. He heard pounding footsteps and saw shadowy figures running from the garrison, a hundred meters away.

From his left, he heard the tailor's shotgun fire, and one of the shadowy figures fell. The gun roared again, and Maurice could see a German soldier get down on one knee to aim at the tailor.

Kuchnir fired at the guard, and Maurice fired his own pistol. Two more Germans fell, but in the dark no one could see how many were left. They could hear more running footsteps from the garrison, and shouts in German.

Maurice threw the gate open. "Go! Get out of here!" Yulia climbed into the seat behind the horse. Maurice heard the reins slapping the horse's back at the same moment he heard another rifle shot. Yulia's head jerked back and she fell into the bed of the wagon. "Shit!" Maurice swore and jumped into the wagon, firing his Luger at the Germans he could not quite see.

The tailor's shotgun spoke one last time, and then the horse neighed and charged through the gate, nearly tipping the wagon over. Maurice pulled it to the right as Kuchnir and Marchuk jumped on. Marchuk had a huge revolver and fired again and again. Kuchnir tried to aim his rifle but fell into the back. A bullet smacked into the side of the wagon and the horse ran even faster.

They rattled over the railroad tracks. Marchuk, sitting beside Maurice, had to hold his fire for fear of hitting Kuchnir, who managed to crouch down in the wagon bed with his rifle barrel resting on the side, and fired toward the German guards behind them. Maurice pulled hard on the reins, turning the horse toward the forest and escape. The horse jumped over the railway track and the wagon followed, tipping to the right. Maurice slammed into Marchuk, who dropped his revolver but managed to grab onto the wagon and stay aboard.

Then they were under the trees, in the protecting shadows of the forest. Maurice gave up trying to steer, trusting the horse to follow a path, any path away from the Germans. He bit his tongue as the wagon shook over ruts and bumps.

"Maurice," Kuchnir called. "She's not dead."

"What?" He twisted in the seat, holding the side of the wagon desperately so he wouldn't be thrown out.

"The girl. She's wounded in the head, but she's still breathing." Maurice looked down, but he could barely see the outline of the girl's body, sprawled on top of bags of flour.

"Try to make her as comfortable as possible." The wagon rocked and tilted again as the horse negotiated a bend in the path. It was slowing down, tired from the panicked flight, and Maurice let it. He did not hear any sounds of pursuit, but he knew the Germans would not let them go. Someone would be punished—most likely, the people who lived in Seredynky. They had all known that, but there were hungry people in other villages.

When the wagon emerged into a clearing, Maurice directed the horse to a different path, leading east, away from their starting point and Maurice's own home.

"Where are you going?" Marchuk asked.

"To the doctor," he answered. "Now keep quiet."

Kuchnir moved the young woman so that she was lying more or less straight, on top of sacks of flour. For the next hour, Maurice directed the horse along paths he could barely see, hoping that he remembered the way to the cabin where UPA's doctor hid.

It took nearly an hour of travel in night so black that the men on the wagon did not realize they had reached the old cabin until the horse stopped in front of a deeper blackness. Marchuk jumped down from the wagon and walked slowly to the shack, stumbling more than once in the dark. He tapped lightly on the door. "Surkis?" he said softly. He tapped again, harder. "Wake up, you lazy Jew."

They saw red light flare through cracks in the cabin's walls. The door creaked open and a man's bearded face appeared. He wore round glasses and a sleeping cap, and he held an oil lantern in front of him. "Who is it?"

"It's me, Semion, Marchuk. We have a friend who needs a doctor."

Surkis hesitated. "It's all right, Doctor. I am Zorenko," said Maurice, using his UPA code name. "Two of our people got shot. One is still alive, but unconscious."

When Surkis stepped outside, the men could see he was wearing a night-shirt, but he also wore pants and old boots. He held the lantern high over the wagon and looked at Yulia lying on the flour bags. Her face was covered in blood and her hair was matted and wet.

I don't even know her last name, Maurice thought. *But that is probably safer for her.*

Surkis touched her throat, feeling for a pulse, and bent over to listen to her breathing. He touched her forehead. "She has a fever," he said.

"Can you help her?" Maurice asked.

"In a hospital, of course. But here? I can only try, with what little I have to work with. Bring her inside, carefully. Don't put any unnecessary strain on her neck and don't touch her head." He went into the cabin.

Maurice lifted Yulia's shoulders and Kuchnir took her under the knees. Careful not to touch her head, Maurice lifted her body over the side of the wagon, where Marchuk took her. Maurice jumped down and then took her legs from Kuchnir, and trying to avoid hurting her further, as well as obstacles on the ground, they brought her into the cabin.

Inside, it was even rougher and more basic than Maurice had imagined. The walls were only thin planks, and the only window was an unglazed opening covered by a shutter. Doctor Surkis opened it and pointed at a high, narrow wooden table covered with a threadbare blanket—his examining table. A small iron stove sat in the corner, next to a narrow cot covered with two rumpled blankets.

They put her down carefully as Surkis hung the lantern from a hook over the table. He covered her with a thin blanket from his bed. "For shock. We need to make sure she's warm."

"It's pretty warm, already," Kuchnir said.

Gingerly, Surkis wiped a wet cloth over her face and head, clearing away blood. Maurice could now see a long, ugly black scar torn through her hair and scalp. "She was lucky," the doctor said. "The bullet did not penetrate the skull, but she is in grave danger. Get me more water from the well and stoke up that stove," he ordered.

Marchuk picked up an old wooden bucket and went outside, while Maurice opened the front door of the wood stove and pushed kindling in, fanning it until it caught. When Marchuk returned with a full bucket, Surkis poured the water into blackened metal pots and put one on top of the stove. While that heated, he dipped a clean cloth into the other pot and wiped the blood off Yulia's face. Then he took scissors from a shelf over the table and cut her hair around the wound, followed by washing the wound itself. Maurice watched the water in the pot turn pink, then red and Surkis dipped the cloth into it again and again.

The cabin began to get hot from the close presence of four men and a woman, and the blazing wood stove. Maurice felt sweat drip down his back.

Marchuk brought over the pot from the stove when it was hot, and Surkis cleaned the wound with the hot water. Maurice watched carefully as the doctor cleaned out the wound until it shone pink in the yellowish light of the lantern, put on a few drops of alcohol to prevent infection and carefully sewed the skin closed. Finally, he put a cloth bandage over the wound and fastened it by wrapping a long strip of cloth around her head.

Maurice and Kuchnir carried her to Surkis' bed. Once they had laid her down and covered her, Maurice realized just how exhausted he felt.

"She will stay here until the evening," Surkis said. "Then take her home. She'll have to stay quiet, resting for several days. Bring me some more food. I'm going to need more bandages, and some alcohol. I'm getting low."

"I'll talk to the commanders," Maurice said. He nodded to his men and they left.

The night was now completely quiet as they rode through the darkness. Maurice could feel exhaustion pulling on his arms and his eyelids, and more than once he started, jerking awake after dozing off. Behind him, both Marchuk and Kuchnir slept, sitting on the bed of the wagon among the sacks and barrels of food.

They returned to Nastaciv, where Maurice directed the wagon to the cemetery beside the church. The other two wagons were already waiting. The others in the group had dug a grave and transferred all the liberated bags and barrels of food to one wagon, so they could arrange Hammer's body on the other as a makeshift hearse. The two teenaged boys stood together, looking sad.

"Where is Yulia?" asked the tailor, who was sitting on the ground beside the wagon.

"With the doctor," Maurice answered.

"What doctor?" he asked, rising to his feet.

"UPA's doctor. You don't need to know any more than that."

"Is she hurt?"

"Her head was grazed by a bullet. She's unconscious, but the doctor is caring for her."

"We can put Hammer to rest," said Spike. He waved to the boys, and together they picked up Hammer's body and as reverently as they could, lowered it into the shallow grave.

"Thank you, brave soldier and patriot," said Maurice, saluting the dead man. "We will all continue to fight so your death will not be in vain. And we will distribute this food to the people of Halychyna, the goal you gave your life for this night."

They shoveled earth into the grave, and as the dawn lightened the eastern sky, departed for their homes.

Maurice collapsed into his bed, feeling a heaviness in his spirit deeper than exhaustion.

Chapter 10:
The heel grinds
Nastaciv, July 1942

Maurice woke at noon the day after the night raid. Hot air came in through the open window and he felt sticky with sweat. After washing, he found his mother in the sweltering barn, tending her still.

"Bad news from the villages around," she said when he came in, without looking up at him. She put more fuel into the little furnace, her brow furrowed. A soft gurgle came from somewhere in the still, and she tapped the copper pipe that led to the first collecting barrel.

The heat from the furnace under the still made Maurice dizzy. "Come outside and tell me." He stepped out and waited for Tekla to finish fussing over her vodka and follow him. Outside, a slight breeze relieved some of the heat of the summer sun.

"What did you hear?" he asked finally, lighting a cigarette.

"Young Yulia Evanyshyn from Yospivka went missing last night. And a man named Yurchik was killed. People buried him here in Nastaciv secretly at night." As she looked up at him, Maurice felt like her eyes were drilling into his head. "You're smoking too much lately."

"Really? I hadn't noticed."

"Where were you all night?"

"It's best if you don't know that." Maurice took one more drag, then threw the half-smoked cigarette to the ground and stomped it with his heel.

"They say the Germans in Seredynky are hopping mad," Tekla said, closing the barn door. Maurice helped her push it closed. "Who says?

"People." She latched the door and walked toward her beet field.

"We better go to the village and find out what people are saying."

"You go. I have work to do here."

Vasyl was sitting at Komorski's café as usual, but outside on the step. "Hey, Maurice," he said as Maurice sat beside him. "Did you hear about Seredynky?"

"Not much. What did you hear?"

"The Germans have burned down five houses and executed three men. They sent their families away, to camps, they say."

Despite the sun beating on the back of his neck, Maurice felt cold. "Why?" came out like a rasp.

"Partisans attacked last night, they say. They killed five German soldiers at the garrison there, so the commander ordered one house burned for each man killed. He shot the fathers of each house himself. One of them had a pretty, young wife and they say he has her in his quarters now, where he's using her for his own sick pleasure." Vasyl spat into the dirt. "Bastards."

Maurice stood, feeling himself tremble from head to foot. He went into Komorski's little house and found the café owner sitting at his own table, his head in his hands. A plain bottle of clear liquid sat on the table, beside a shot glass. "Is it true what they're saying about Seredynky?" Maurice asked.

Komorski looked pale. He smoothed his hair and spoke to the table. "The Germans set the first house on fire at dawn. They didn't even bother giving the people inside a warning to get out. They shot the father in front of his three children."

"How do you know this?"

"The brother of one of the men shot came down here a few hours ago. His name was Loboda, and he was my cousin." With shaking hands, Komorski poured a shot from the bottle, slopping some of the homemade whiskey onto the table. He threw the drink into his mouth and swallowed. He tried to pour another shot, but his hands could not keep the bottle's mouth over the glass. Maurice took the bottle and poured for him.

"Yurchik was killed and buried secretly last night, too," Komorski continued. "He lived here, in this village. He was my friend. It won't take the Germans long to work out the connection." He looked up, finally, at Maurice. "Are they going to come here, Maurice? How many houses will they burn in Nastaciv? How many men will they shoot? How many girls are they going to rape?"

He pushed the bottle to Maurice. "No, thank you," Maurice said. He nearly ran out of the café to Zazulak's house.

But he could not find Zazulak anywhere in the village, and two hours later, Maurice's shirt was soaked with sweat. He returned home and refused to tell his family anything. All night he sat in front of his window, watching and listening for signs of Germans.

For the next several weeks, Maurice remained close to home—which pleased his mother, because there was plenty of work to do on a farm in the summer. He fretted over his mother every evening that she pulled her wagon to the village to sell vodka to the Germans. Only at midnight would he dare venture to the collection points for the coded messages from UPA.

Some of them were news from the front.
Germans moving deep into southeast. Likely target: Caucasus oil fields.

Panzer Army takes Voronezh, but is not moving farther.

Red Army offensive at Rzhev failed. Three armies destroyed.

German 6th and 4th Panzer Armies driving toward Stalingrad. With Romanian and Hungarian auxiliaries, they have over a million men. Predict fall of Stalingrad in weeks.

Others concerned UPA operations.
UPA captured four railway coaches at Shepetkivka. Arming units in Khmelnytskyi Oblast

Food stores captured, distributed in Kozova

Especially troubling were reports of fighting among Ukrainians.
OUN-B units massacre 5 UPA men in Volhynia

Ukrainian communist partisans raided UPA

OUN-M betrayed OUN-B units to Germans in Zhytomyr

There were reports of fighting between Bandera's armed groups and ethnic Poles in Volhynia and Halychyna, areas long disputed between Ukrainians and Poles.
OUN-B burns Polish village
OUN-B massacred Jewish village

Zazulak remained out of sight for three days. On the fourth evening after the night raid, Maurice found him in the machine shop next to his house in the evening. "Where have you been?" he demanded.

Zazulak put tools into a box and ushered Maurice outside. As he locked the door, he said "Fixing the mess you left behind. Did you get Yulia home?"

"Day before yesterday. What a botched operation."

"Not really. One lost, one wounded—you got off lightly." Zazulak lit a cigarette and gave one to Maurice. "It's too bad about Hammer, though."

"What about the families the Germans took revenge on the next day?"

"That's what I meant about fixing your mess. I led another large, experienced UPA unit. We wiped out that garrison. I lost three men doing it."

"My god! What will the Germans do about that?"

"Think twice about attacking innocents. Don't worry—we left no trace, and not a German left alive. Their replacements have nothing to go on."

"I hope you're right." As Zazulak turned to leave for home, Maurice asked him about the problem that bothered him most. "I'm getting reports about Bandera's branch of the Organization of Ukrainian Nationalists."

"Yes. Bandera wants to rid Ukraine of communists, Poles and Jews as well as Germans."

"They're also killing other Ukrainians. People in UPA."

"It's a war, Maurice. What else can I say?"

"A war of four sides?"

"Maybe fewer, soon. Bulba-Borovets has been talking about merging UPA, OUN-B and OUN-M into one united force. But Bandera won't do it unless he's in charge."

In September, Maurice accepted an offer to teach at the local Ridna Shkola, or elementary school. Because there were few teachers and fewer resources, he taught a group that ranged from ages eight to twelve. The Polish government had closed Ukrainian schools more than once during the 1930s, and now the war had interrupted the children's education again.

Many of the children who showed up that first day had not set foot in a classroom for over a year.

Sitting in their little wooden desks, some looked up at him with wonder. Others giggled at the back of the room. He introduced himself, feeling a little ridiculous. He already knew many of the children as neighbours and cousins. Nastaciv was a tiny village, after all.

As the children came back day after day—most of them, anyway, most school days—Maurice wondered what it would be like to teach during peacetime. He had trouble concentrating on the lessons, and he knew his pupils had more elemental issues on their minds than reading and arithmetic.

On a Tuesday in the second week of class, Maurice saw an empty desk. Leon, the tall teenager who had helped on the night raid in the summer, was missing. His ten-year-old sister, Alina, sat with her head hanging over her desk. Her pigtails hung over her face. As he stepped closer, Maurice could see tears dripping onto the textbook on the desk.

He squatted beside her. "What's wrong, Alina?"

A sob made her shoulders heave and more tears splashed onto the book. Maurice put his hand on her back, gently. Other students looked at them, faces grave. "Where is your brother, Leon?" Alina's only answer was another sob, which turned into a long wail. Her shoulders shook. Maurice put his arm around her, squeezing her gently in a futile effort to calm the girl.

"They took him away last night," said another girl, Yana, who was twelve.

Maurice's throat was dry. "Who took him?"

"The Germans," said a boy, Alexei, also twelve. "A Gestapo truck came in the middle of the night. They took him and beat his father. He cannot work today."

At that, Alina wailed again. Maurice took her into his arms, patting the back of her head. He had never felt so useless. There was nothing he could say.

In the evenings, he read, transcribed and compiled reports from his area, and others relayed from farther east.

> *German Army surrounded village near Zhitomyr, machine-gunned houses. Took food and fuel supplies, then burned all the houses. No one left alive.*

> *100 young men taken from Ternopyl, sent west in cattle cars to work in German factories.*

> *Koch decreed that those refusing to work for Germans on farms or in factories are saboteurs. They shot 24 people in Kyiv in September.*

> *Food supplies non-existent in Kyiv. Women arrested for traveling to village market.*

The Gestapo arrested Kuchnir in November. Who tipped them off to his being in UPA, no one could say. He endured four days of torture without giving up his UPA contacts.

On the fifth day, German soldiers hung Kuchnir's naked body upside down from a scaffold in the middle of the village.

At midnight, Maurice and Zazulak went to the village to give Kuchnir some dignity. Maurice stopped when he saw the body as if someone had just punched him in the gut. He could not take another step forward, but could not tear his eyes from the scene.

Kuchnir's naked body swung from a gibbet the Germans had built. Maurice and Zazulak could tell that both his legs had been broken, because while his feet touched the ground, not moving, the body swayed slightly in the breeze. The tops of the legs moved with the body, but at breaks in the thighs, the bottoms did not move.

"Come on, let's cut him down," said Zazulak, his voice hoarse.

Maurice had seen death many times on the battlefield, men's bodies mutilated and dismembered by bullets and bombs, but that did not prepare him for the calculated brutality that had been applied to Kuchnir. As he got closer, he saw that his friend hung not by a rope, but by a wire looped around his neck. It had eaten into the skin, eroding a horrible, oozing scar. More scars ran down his shaved head, his back and his arms. His face was frozen forever in an expression of agony, one eye open, looking upward. The other was an empty, black socket, gore trailing down over the cheek.

Maurice felt the tears on his face as he held the body up by the waist. Zazulak cut the wire, cursing under his breath. They put the body as gently as they could into a wheelbarrow Zazulak had brought, and quietly retreated to the cemetery where Fence and Kuchnir's brother waited. The younger Kuchnir said a prayer as Fence and Maurice filled in the shallow grave.

When they were done, Zazulak gave each of them a cigarette. "You had better get out of here now," he told the younger Kuchnir.

"I'm planning to join UPA in Volhynia," he answered, wiping his face. He was a handsome young man, short and slight with a thick mop of hair. Maurice did not know him well, and guessed he was maybe eighteen years old. "Maybe I can join a partisan unit, one that lives in the forest, out of sight."

"Good idea," Zazulak agreed. "Keep out of sight of the Germans. But in Volhynia, you'll have to watch out for the communists and the Poles as well as the fucking Germans."

Young Kuchnir finished his cigarette and slung a pack onto his back. He put the strap of a rifle over one shoulder, waved to the little group and disappeared into the night.

Maurice turned away from the others without a word, wondering whether he would one day get used to seeing his friends brutally killed. *I hope not, but I think it's inevitable.*

Chapter 11: Meeting in the snow

January, 1943

The winter of 1943 was not as cold as 1942, when oil froze in Panzer engines, but January nights were bitter. Driving a single-horse sleigh through the forest at night, Maurice pulled his fur hat lower on his head and the collar of his coat higher.

He was returning by horse-cart from a village called Prosova, in the eastern part of his range. He had left a little before sunset. No one would want to be out on such a cold night, and the Germans had long before learned not to venture at night into the countryside. The Ukrainian Insurgent Army lived deep in the forests and swamps, supported by willing donations of locals. And then there was the rival OUN-B, the nationalists led by Stepan Bandera, who had no mercy for soldiers, agents, spies and collaborators of either Nazi Germany or the USSR.

The snow beside the sleigh tracks was deep and the setting sun turned the clear, distant sky a vivid yellow in the west. When he looked back over his shoulder, he could see white stars against the deep purple-blue sky.

Maurice shivered under his thick fleece blankets and flicked the reins to urge the horse to go a little faster. He steered toward trees, keeping to the paths known to the locals. Still, Maurice knew that their security depended on adherence to the rules of secrecy and stealth. They worked in separate units, communicated only in the stefetka code and used only code names. Maurice did not even know the real name, nor the face of his superior officer, and he had never met most of the agents who reported to him.

Every move was fraught with multiple risks: risks of being observed by one of the enemies; of their intelligence being faked; of being killed by the Germans, the Communists or by mistake by partisans. Maurice shivered again.

Maurice's heart began to pound when he saw a slim shape on a big, black horse coming straight toward him through the trees, along a path that crossed his. Maurice took his pistol from its holster and held it under the blanket, then chucked the reins to speed up his horse so that he would reach the path intersection before the rider.

Just as the last daylight faded, Maurice reined in so that his sleigh blocked the intersecting path. The rider stopped when he could actually see his face. It was a young boy, maybe thirteen or fourteen years old. "Good evening, sir," he said in a shaky voice.

"You're out late tonight," Maurice said, and he knew he did not sound friendly. He was nervous, himself. Why was a young boy out after curfews? "Where are you going?"

"To see my uncle," said the boy, trembling. Maurice became more curious. Why was this boy being evasive? Why was he so afraid? He must have been able to tell that Maurice was not a German officer.

"Where does your uncle live?"

The boy hesitated. "In ... in Mykulynci." The town was about five kilometres away, but still, why was a young boy traveling alone at night? Maurice started to get the feeling that the boy thought he was doing something heroic.

"You had better tell me what you're doing," Maurice said in a softer tone. Not friendly, but not unfriendly, either.

"What do you mean?"

"I mean, tell me the real reason you're travelling at night when there are strict curfews. It's not safe."

"I'm not afraid," said the boy, looking around. But the only way forward was blocked by Maurice's sleigh, and the snow was too deep for the horse to pass around it.

"Why are you going to Mykulynci?" Maurice asked again.

"I told you, to see my uncle."

"What's his name?"

"I don't see why I should be telling you anything. I don't even know who you are!"

"You don't need to know who I am. But I know who you are," Maurice lied. "And I know you're much too young to be doing what you're trying to do. Who are you going to see?"

"I'm not too young to love my country!"

"This is not a game." Maurice leaned close to the boy, his voice a growl. "This is a war between grown-up men, and children who get involved always get killed." Maurice decided to change tactics. "Listen, my friend, I know what you're trying to do. But think how your mother would feel if you were hurt — or worse. And what if you fell into German hands?"

"I'm not afraid of the Germans! We rule the night!"

"'We'? Who are 'we'?"

The boy's eyes widened and he looked around again. He realized he had made a serious mistake.

Maurice leaned close. "Which unit are you with?" he whispered. When the boy hesitated, he said "Come on, you can trust me. I'm a Ukrainian, not a German. I love my country, too."

"Can I really trust you?"

"Oh, yes. I'm friendly to ... our side." Maurice wished he could say more, but the less the boy knew, the safer he would be.

The boy leaned closer and whispered "I'm bringing a message to Mr. Stefaniuk in Mykulynci. It's from a man named ... 'Half-Moon.'"

"Half-Moon" was the code name of one of Maurice's agents, one of the few he knew personally. Maxim Tanshysyn was a lazy old bureaucrat who was never on time, nor were his reports ever complete. Now he was sending children to do his work for him. "What sort of message?"

"I don't know. I was told to put the message directly into the hands of Mr. Stefaniuk." The boy pulled a slip of paper from a pocket, but held it close to his chest.

"I know Mr. Stefaniuk myself. I'll get the message to him. I know all the people involved in this. I'm a friend of ... our organization. Your duty is to look after your family and not to endanger any of your comrades. And someone your age, out here, is going to draw a lot of attention from the enemy. If you get caught, you'll endanger everyone that you know. Is that what you want?"

Maurice could see that the boy was thinking about it, and that he was a lot more scared than he had been at first. He suddenly thrust the paper to Maurice. "I'm trusting you." Without another word, he turned the horse around carefully and retreated down the path. In seconds, his shadow had melted into the forest.

Maurice opened the note. In the dim moonlight, he could barely make out rows of numbers. It was the stefetka code, all right. Half-Moon was going to get it.

But now, he had to make another detour before returning home, to bring the message to Stefaniuk in Mykulinci.

The next day was a Sunday, but Maurice did not go to church. He hitched the sleigh and set off for "Half-Moon's" home as the sun turned the thin, high clouds red and gold. The air was still and quiet and bit at his nostrils with every breath. The wind of the night before had polished the surface of the snow in the fields so that it reflected the low sunlight like the surface of water. Maurice pulled a thick fleece blanket around his shoulders and another over his knees and adjusted the collar of his coat, but he was warm as the horse trotted along the packed snow of the road to Ternopyl.

He arrived at "Half Moon's" two-storey house near the southern end of the city just as the man and his wife were returning from church. They were stamping the snow off their boots as Maurice reined in at their garden gate. "Maxim," he called, striding up the cleared front path. Half-Moon, a short, fat man with thick glasses, turned toward Maurice as his wife, even shorter and fatter, stepped into the big, luxurious house.

"Maurice Bury!" Maxim called in surprise. "What brings you here today?" He blinked, confused, his watery eyes enlarged to ridiculous proportions by his glasses.

"I need to talk to you," Maurice said. He took the man's elbow in his hand and lowered his voice. "Half-Moon."

Maxim started, his whole body shaking. He blinked and swallowed, then looked up and down the street. His neighbours were returning from church, too, hurrying into their houses out of the cold or leading horses into barns and carriage-houses. "What is it?"

"Someplace private," Maurice said.

Maxim swallowed again. "All right, come in. I have a room where we can talk. Put your horse in my carriage-house."

Maurice led the horse into the little stable beside Maxim's house, unhitched it from the sleigh and gave it some hay from Maxim's stores. He hurried into the house, feeling the chill of the air creeping up his arms and down his chest. Maxim's fat wife, Olena, let him into the kitchen, took his coat and boots, and gave him a cup of tea on a saucer. "Maxim is in the front room," she said, then turned away to busy herself with preparing Sunday lunch.

Careful not to spill his tea, Maurice padded in his stocking feet down a short hallway hung with photographs of Maxim Tanshysyn with men in suits, even one with a German in a major's uniform.

Maxim, wearing a suit that struggled to cover his round belly, was scooping coal into a small iron stove in the corner of a small room that he used as a study. It had an ice-crusted window, a desk, a sagging leather easy chair and a smaller wooden one. The stove was not yet giving off heat, and Maurice was glad that he had worn his Sunday jacket that day.

Maxim shut the stove and stood. He was a short man with just a ring of dark hair around his head. He had a round face and pudgy, soft hands, the result of a job in city administration that required no physical labour, little movement but plenty of opportunity for bribes. Maurice knew he had a married daughter and a grandchild, and that his son-in-law had been drafted into the Red Army like him. No one had heard from him since June of 1941.

Maurice put his tea cup on the desk and sat in the leather chair. Maxim did not seem happy about that, but did not say anything. He frowned, instead, and sat heavily on the wooden chair.

"Are you finding your duties too difficult, Maxim?" Maurice asked, his voice calm and his face unreadable.

"N-no," Maxim answered. He frowned more deeply. "Is something wrong?"

Maurice took a slip of paper from his jacket pocket and held it up in front of Maxim's face. It was only a foot away in the small room. "Recognize this?" It was the slip with the coded message that Maurice had taken from the boy in the forest the night before.

Maxim went pale and swallowed again. "You should not have brought that here, Maurice," he whispered.

"That's 'Captain Zorenko' to you," Maurice growled.

Maxim went even paler. His hands began to shake. "Maurice! Do not use words like that in my house, please," he whispered.

"So now you're careful about security, about secrecy, but your scruples don't prevent you from giving secret messages to children and sending them to do your work for you. You put that boy in danger, you lazy idiot. You put us all in danger."

"I'm sorry, Maurice," Maxim stammered.

"Sorry? I should shoot you right now." He did not say he had not brought a gun with him.

Maxim's whole body began to shake. "No, please! I have a wife, I have grandchildren. I am loyal to the cause, Maurice—I mean, captain!" He slid out of the chair onto his knees in front of Maurice. "I will never do it again," he went on, his whispers getting hoarse. "From now on, I will take all the messages to the drop points myself."

"So? You should have been doing that all along, like everyone else. There is no excuse. You are a liability to us. A risk." Maurice stood and put his right hand into his empty jacket pocket.

Maxim gasped, then threw himself face-down on the floor. "Please, Captain, I am sorry. I will do better. I will work even harder to make up for this mistake." He began to sob, but quietly—he did not want his wife to hear.

"What does your wife know about us?" Maurice asked.

"Nothing, nothing, not a single thing, I swear. I have been very careful, completely secret."

"Who else has run messages for you?"

"No one. Just young Stepan, no one else. He is very trustworthy, very smart. That's why I trusted him with my messages."

"I should still shoot you," Maurice said. But he was getting weary of tormenting Maxim Tanshysyn, even though he was a greedy, lazy good-for-nothing.

"Please, please Maurice. Think of my wife, my family." He turned so he could look up at Maurice from the floor, and Maurice saw his face was wet with tears. His glasses had slipped down his nose and he peered fuzzily up at Maurice.

"You need to be punished, Maxim, so you remember this lesson." Some of the fear left Maxim's expression at those words. He started to get up. "No, stay on the ground," Maurice ordered. "I am going to punish you." Inspiration flashed in Maurice's mind. "You're going to do something you haven't done in years, probably in decades. You're going to do push-ups."

Maxim's jaw dropped in a combination of relief, confusion and fear. "What?"

"That's right, you lazy clod. Twenty push-ups. Right now!" he shouted.

"But—but Maurice, I'm too old for that—"

Maurice reached into his pocket again. "You're right. I'll just shoot you, after all."

"No!" Maxim lay flat again, put his hands beside his shoulders and tried to brace his feet on the wooden floor. He wore slippers, which made it difficult, but he kicked them off and strained to lift his overweight body from the floor.

"That's a girl's push-up," Maurice said. "Get your ass off the ground."

Maxim lifted his rear end high, and then his arms collapsed and he went down to the floor hard. "That's one, if a shitty one," Maurice said. "Nineteen to go."

Maxim strained and pushed himself up again, butt high. He lowered himself again, right to the floor. "Your chin should touch the floor on the way down, but nothing else," Maurice said. "Do it properly or I won't count them."

Maxim pushed himself up, then lowered himself with shaking arms but did not rest on the floor. He did another proper push-up, puffing and sweating, then lowered himself and asked "Can I take off my jacket?"

"All right. But get right back to it, or I will shoot you." It's a good thing I did not bring my gun, he thought I'm so tempted to shoot him.

Maxim rose to his knees, trembling, and slid his jacket off his narrow shoulders. He smoothed it on the seat of the wooden chair, glanced at Maurice, licked his lips, sighed and sank back to the floor. He put his hands next to his shoulders again and strained to lift himself.

By the time he got to ten, Maxim's arms were shaking and his breath wheezed. Sweat dripped from his face onto the floor and stained his Sunday shirt.

Maurice slumped in the leather chair, bored. I have things to do. When Maxim got to fifteen, he collapsed with a groan, arms and legs splayed wide like a starfish. "One more, Maxim," Maurice said, rising.

Maxim took two deep breaths, placed his hands and feet and gave a last mighty push. His body rose and then fell. He rolled over onto his back and looked at Maurice, his face and body drenched. The stove was just starting to give off some heat, but Maurice had had enough.

"Don't forget this," he said. He carried his tea cup back to the kitchen, where Olena looked at him with fear on her face. She did not say anything, just stood beside the sink, holding a pot. "Thank you for the tea," Maurice told her, then put on his boots and coat and left.

Maurice stepped into his mother's kitchen and pulled off his gloves, but Hanya stopped him. "Zazulak came by." Her face was grave, worried. "He wants you to go see him as soon as you can."

That could only mean bad news, Maurice knew. "What's going on?"

"I don't know. He just said he had to talk to you as soon as possible."

Maurice sighed, pulled his gloves back on and went back outside. Zazulak's house was at least fifteen minutes away on foot, but Maurice decided against hitching up the sleigh yet again that day. He began to question his decision, though, as the cold deepened. He began an awkward jog on the packed snow, and by the time he reached Zazulak, he was out of breath.

Zazulak took Maurice into the machine shop behind his house. "Big changes, Maurice," he said. He looked excited, almost happy. "We have new leadership that's going to get a lot more aggressive against the Germans, and the communists and Poles, too."

"What are you talking about?" Maurice said, hoping the alarm he felt did not find its way into his voice.

"Bandera has taken over UPA."

"That maniac? I thought he was in prison in Berlin."

"He is, but he's still communicating through OUN-B," the Organization of Ukrainian Nationalists, Bandera wing. "He has proclaimed the formation of the Ukrainian Insurgent Army under OUN, using Bulba's units."

"What does Taras Bulba say about that?" Maurice asked, referring to Taras Bulba- Borovets, the founder of the original Ukrainian Insurgent Army in 1941 to resist German exploitation.

"He's out. Listen, Maurice, this is an army. And in an army, you follow orders or you get shot."

"I know what an army is about, Zazulak. I fought in one, against the Germans, remember? You never did."

"Then you know what I'm talking about. We're fighting under Stepan Bandera now."

"Bandera is a maniac. He hates Jews more than Hitler does and his men have been killing more Poles than Germans."

"We have a better chance for an independent Ukraine under Bandera than anyone else. OUN-B is ten times the size of Bulba's army. Most of UPA's units have already joined Bandera."

"Or been forced to," Maurice interrupted.

Zazulak swept his hand to brush away Maurice's comment. "It doesn't matter. Our group is now part of Bandera's UPA. Nothing else changes, Maurice, at least not for now. You keep working intelligence. And come the spring, I think we can expect to see some real action."

What do I do now? Maurice wondered as he trudged home. Clouds had covered the sky and snow began to fall, wet and heavy flakes.

By the time he reached his mother's house again, he knew there was no alternative. He had to fight for Ukraine. Now, that meant his ally was Stepan Bandera's Organization of Ukrainian Nationalists.

At least there will be a little more unity among Ukrainians. I hope.

Chapter 12: Kalush

August 1943

"We need you in Kalush. Be there in three days." Zazulak pressed a slip of paper into Maurice's hand.

Maurice unfolded it. An address in Kalush.

"Why Kalush?"

"Because the Russians are coming back, Maurice. The city is mostly empty. The Soviets sent all the Poles to Siberia in 1939. The Germans took most of the Jews away to their 'resettlement camps' and killed the rest. Ukrainians moved in while the Germans were there, but the town is still half-empty, and now the Soviets are sending their agents in. They're up to something and the Red Army won't be far behind."

Maurice nodded. The Red Army had been pushing the Germans back since destroying the 6th Army and the 43 Panzer Army at Stalingrad in February 1943. The following summer, the Germans moved nearly a million men, three thousand tanks, over two thousand aircraft and nearly ten thousand heavy guns, cannons and mortars in an effort to encircle the "Kursk salient," a 300-kilometre westward bulge in the front lines. Field Marshal Erich von Manstein's plan was the classic "pincer movement," which had worked so well in 1941. The German forces were penetrating from the north and the south until they met at the city of Kursk, encircling and capturing the Soviet army group, the Central Front.

The plan failed. Soviet and British intelligence warned Moscow of Germany's plan, and the Red Army commandeered more than 300,000 civilians to help prepare for the attack. They spent the months from May to July preparing, secretly moving men, guns and aircraft to meet the German offensive. When the Germans finally attacked after two months of delays, they found successive defensive belts of minefields, trenches and fortifications. Operation Citadel, the last German offensive on the Eastern Front, stalled far from its objective. And while Soviet losses were about double those of Germany's, losing a quarter of a million experienced soldiers was a blow the Third Reich would never recover from. After Kursk, the story of the Eastern Front was the story of German retreat.

"If we're going to make Ukraine free, we need Kalush," Zazulak said. "We need you to help coordinate intelligence."

"But it's a hundred kilometres away. Who is going to look after my mother and sister? What about the farm?"

Zazulak pierced him with a look from under his bushy eyebrows. "A free Ukraine is more important than any single family or farm." He sighed. "I'll keep an eye on them. We'll have a few boys to help with the farm, too."

"But—"

"Kalush. Three days." Zazulak turned away, focused on the next task. "That's an order."

Three days later, Maurice knocked on the door of a large stone house on a quiet street off Kalush's main square. He checked the address on the paper again. The right place. He tore the paper into little pieces and let the breeze scatter them.

He looked up and down the street. Kalush indeed seemed half empty. There were only a handful of people in the square and there was no traffic on the street. On the other hand, the town seemed to be undamaged by the war. There had been no, or very little fighting there, apparently.

Even the Germans seemed complacent. The swastika floated over the town hall, and a single guard in a grey uniform stood outside, smoking.

Maurice knocked on the door again. Waiting made him nervous. He had no business in Kalush, nothing that the Gestapo would accept as legitimate, anyway.

After a minute-long eternity, a slender blond woman opened the door. She looked at him, but did not say anything.

"Hello," Maurice stammered. "Were you expecting me?"

"Was I?"

Maurice took a breath. "Bread and salt," he said. The password.

The blond woman's expression changed from curious to worried. She swallowed but stepped back from the door. "Come in," she said.

Maurice glanced once more up and down the street, picked up his bag and stepped across the threshold. The woman closed the door and recited the password rejoinder: "To you and your family."

She led him to the kitchen, which held a wooden table and a wood stove. "Would you like some tea?"

Maurice would have preferred vodka, but he said "Yes, please."

He sat down. "My name is Maurice."

"Katerina."

Maurice took a deep breath. *If she's not one of us, this could mean my death. Be careful, Maurice.* "They also call me 'Zorenko.'"

Katerina stoked the fire in the stove, replaced the iron cover and put a kettle on it. "I know, 'little star.' You don't look so little to me, though.'"

"Um, no, I'm not actually little, it's just ... a nickname."

Katerina sat down at the table opposite Maurice. She reached forward and patted his hand, which was resting on the table top. "Relax, little star. I am javor, the maple tree."

Maurice nearly choked. "You're javor? I am sorry, I, I,..."

"You were expecting a man?"

"Of course, yes." Maurice looked directly into Katerina's eyes. He liked the little crinkles at the corners and the way her lips parted slightly so they could turn into either a smile or a sneer, depending on what he said next.

"Women are often better than men in intelligence," she said.

"Because they're smarter than men." He was careful to leave the inflection, the question, out of the sentence.

"Every time that I've found," she answered. Her mouth refused to smile.

"So, does that make you the smartest person in Kalush?"

Her eyes narrowed and she let go of his hand. "In Halychyna," she answered, meaning the entire region that included Kalush and Ternopyl.

"I knew that when I saw you," Maurice said.

The kettle whistled. Katerina stood, and Maurice watched her make tea.

"Where did you find lemons in wartime?" he asked as she set two cups on the table.

She smiled and winked. "I told you, I'm smart."

Her smile faded. "The first thing we need to do is set you up with a reason to be here. What are your skills? What can you do?"

"I was a teacher at the Ridna Shkola in Nastaciv."

"Good!" She patted his hand again. "The school here has openings for teachers. I know the headmaster. I can get you in."

"The headmaster—is he ... one of us?"

She tilted her head. "You know better than to ask that kind of question, Zorenko."

"And where will I live?"

"This house is much too big for me alone," she said. She smiled and winked, and Maurice's heart pounded in his chest. "Come on, I'll show you a bedroom."

Katerina installed him in a small bedroom on the top floor of the house. It had a single bed, a stand with a washbasin and ewer, a wooden wardrobe, a writing table and a chair. A coal-oil lamp stood on the table.

"You can stay here as long as we need you in Kalush," she said. "Settle in and come downstairs at five."

Two hours later, Maurice had washed, shaved and changed his clothes. Katerina had put a long, colourful apron over her dress and tied her hair back with an embroidered kerchief. She turned from the stove, where a pan seared sausages and scrambled eggs, and put two plates on the table. She moved the pan away from the heat and sliced a loaf of rye bread, then put the slices on another plate and put it on the table. "Hungry?" she asked.

"Famished."

"Then, eat!" She smiled and sat down behind one of the plates. Maurice sat at the other plate, beside her. The sausage was delicious, the bread fresh from the morning. "No shortages here?" he asked.

"The Germans take most of the eggs, most of the vegetables and meat. The only thing they leave us are sausages, some bread, a few other scraps. Oh, and vodka."

"Are there many Germans here in the city?"

"Just a small garrison that rotates through here. Most of the time, it's Romanian or Hungarian troops. But more Ukrainians moved here since 1939 than anyone else, so the city is mostly Ukrainian now."

"You mean, since the Poles and Jews left."

"Since the Russians took most of the Poles to Siberia, and the Germans murdered all the Jews, yes. There's still a lot of empty room in Kalush. Houses are worth almost nothing now. Ukrainians lost their livelihoods, but at least most of us didn't lose our lives."

"As long as we give everything to Germany."

"As long as we kneel to *der Fuhrer*."

"So, what's the plan?"

"I thought that's why they sent you," Katerina said.

"Germany and Russia are going to wear each other down until they both collapse. Our job is to make sure that Ukraine is ready to declare independence, and to be a free country when that happens," said Maurice. "What is ready in Kalush?"

Katerina leaned close, as if afraid someone could overhear. But they were alone in the house. "We have people ready to step in to the administrative departments, the police and the armoury. All we need is the word."

Maurice looked into Katerina's clear blue eyes and saw a fire burning there, and behind that, a strength like steel.

Katerina spent the next day orienting Maurice to Kalush. She led him along the street that followed the river to show him the layout of the city, but mostly so that no one could overhear them.

Katerina pointed out the city hall, the key fire halls, the Orthodox Church. "That used to be a Polish church until 1939. Then Stalin declared that there were officially no more Poles in Kalush, but we couldn't use it as a church because the communists outlawed all religions but communism. The Germans let us open the church. A small mercy when they took away so many as slaves. "

"Were you born here?" Maurice asked.

"No," she said, but nothing more about herself. A good spy, Maurice thought.

"The Organization of Ukrainian Nationalists is getting ready to proclaim an independent Ukrainian state. My job is to coordinate activities here, so that we can seize control of key positions immediately: water, fire department, electrical grid, city administration, police and most importantly, the armoury," Maurice said.

Katerina gave Maurice her arm, then led him away from a group of people gathering in the city square. They walked down a tree-lined lane. Katerina put her head on Maurice's shoulder, like a lover.

"Our people, OUN and UPA members, are in second- and third-level positions throughout the city. But we have to be careful—there are a lot of Communists, too. Some are sympathizers with the USSR, communists from before the war. And the NKVD has been sending a lot of spies in, too."

"Do we know who the spies are?"

"Some of them. And some of them know who some of us are, no doubt."

"Besides leaders, do we have some rough-and-ready boys when the fighting starts?"

"Lots. The police are all on our side, except for the new chief the Germans appointed."

"I need to meet these men," Maurice said.

"What makes you sure they're all men?"

Maurice smiled at her. "Aren't they?"

Katerina scowled. "Yes." She punched him on the shoulder. It hurt.

This was the plan that Volivets had outlined for Zorenko: When the Organization of Ukrainian

Nationals, the government-in-exile, proclaimed the Ukrainian State, the men they had placed in key posts would arrest their superiors and take charge of the important elements of the infrastructure: police, power, security forces, electrical grid, waterworks, highways, city council, schools. OUN would have effective control of all the organs of the state.

But as Maurice ate bread and drank tea on his second morning at Katerina's house, he heard a knock at the door.

Katerina went alone to answer. Sitting in the kitchen, Maurice heard a whiny, nasal voice lisp questions without an opening pleasantry.

"You have a new tenant?" Maurice knew no one at the door could see him in the kitchen, but he heard every word and knew that if he moved, he would betray himself as well as Katerina.

"Yes, sir. To help pay the rent." Maurice relaxed. Katerina was not going to try to hide him, after all.

"The rent is charged per person, not per housing unit, miss." The Director's voice was thin, whiny and lisping. "He did not come from Kalush, though." It was not a question.

How did he hear this so quickly? Maurice wondered. *Who is watching this house?*

"No, sir. He came from Ternopyl, I believe."

"His profession? How does he propose to pay his rent?"

"I believe he is ... he is a teacher. A schoolteacher."

"A schoolteacher. Well, the Ridna Shkola needs some new teachers. Is that why he moved from Ternopyl?"

"I believe so, sir."

Her voice held just the right combination of nervousness and deference to be convincing, Maurice noted. But he and she had practiced these answers the night before.

"His name?" the Director asked.

"Bury. Maurice Bury. From Ternopyl."

"May I meet him?"

"Yes, of course, comrade. Maurice!" she called. Maurice went to the hallway. Katerina stood beside the open front door. On the doorstep stood a short man with thick receding chin and wire-rim glasses. He wore the grey and black uniform of German-appointed civic administrators. He held open a leather-bound notebook in one hand, and in the other a pencil poised to make a black mark. He squinted into the gloom to make out Maurice.

"You come from Ternopyl?" he asked.

"Yes, sir. Pleased to meet you." Maurice held out his hand to shake, but the Director ignored it.

"Papers? From the *generalgouvernement* offices in Ternopyl?"

Maurice pulled a card and a small slip of paper from an inner pocket. The card was his authentic certification as a school teacher in Ternopyl, signed by Professor Posmychuk. The slightly larger, folded slip was a travel authorization from UPA's best forger. Maurice remembered to breathe normally as the Director squinted at it, but he could hear his pulse in his ears.

After what felt like an hour, the Director thrust the slip back at Maurice. "Very well. The rent is 10 kopeks per week."

Maurice had expected that, but he knew that that amount included five kopeks that went directly into the Director's own pocket. "That seems very high," he said.

The Director's eyes flared open and his already thin lips nearly disappeared. Katerina said, "Maurice, we talked about this."

"Ten kopeks per week is the rent. Otherwise, you can go back to Ternopyl," said the Director.

Maurice sighed, reached into his pocket and drew a ten-kopek note. The Director took it, put it in a pocket of his notebook, snapped the notebook closed and from a pocket took out a small receipt book. He filled out the receipt and gave Maurice the carbon-copy, staining his own fingers in the process. He put away the receipt book, tucked his chewed pencil into his breast pocket and wiped his blackened fingertips with a white handkerchief. "I will be back next Thursday for the rent. Ten kopeks. I suggest you secure a job by then."

On the next Monday, Katerina took Maurice to the local Ridna Shkola. In the office, she introduced him to Mr. Bylih, the headmaster. "Mr. Bury, here, has a number of years' experience as a teacher in Ternopyl," she said.

Mr. Bylih was a frail looking man with a large, bald head and watery brown eyes. His grey suit was tattered and his wooden desk was scarred. One eye was clouded and his hands shook.

Still, he did not look convinced. "What did you teach?"

"Third to fifth years," Maurice answered. He knew that the best cover stories were true stories.

"Use the subjunctive mode," said Mr. Bylih.

"If I were to try to deceive you, headmaster, I would not be applying for a job as a simple schoolteacher."

Mr. Bylih nodded. "Good enough. You can start on Wednesday with the third year students. Teach them grammar, history and geography. And do your best not to get killed."

"Headmaster Bylih?" the words had stabbed Maurice in the heart.

"The last three teachers all died. Sent to war for the Red Army, arrested by the Nazis, executed by communist agents. If you go, too, the children will have been without a teacher for three years. These three years are very important for young minds."

Maurice's mouth was dry. "Yes, headmaster. Thank you."

Two days later, he watched twenty children file into the classroom. Sunlight glared off the blackboards and illuminated the gouges in the hardwood floor. The children sat at their desks and watched him warily as he wrote his name on the blackboard: "Mr. Bury."

He turned and surveyed the classroom. They were quiet, looking at him with an expression that struck Maurice as a kind of dismissive pity. No wonder. They don't expect me to live much longer.

"Good morning, class," he said, forcing himself to smile. "I'm going to start with the history of Ukraine."

Katerina was waiting for him on the steps of the schoolhouse after his first day. "Don't you have to be at work?"

"I told the administrator that I had to help orient you to the city," she said. "They don't argue with me."

Under the guise of showing Maurice the city, Katerina took him to meet "our people." They usually met outside a cafe or church, and then they would walk while talking.

The first was a grey-haired man named Oleh Sewchuk. "He is the assistant manager of the city works department," said Katerina.

"Such as it is," Sewchuk said. "Most of our equipment and of course all the men were taken either by the Russians or the Germans. We have a few men with shovels to fix potholes or clear the sewers, but that's it."

"Are you ready for the signal?" Maurice asked.

"What signal?"

"You'll know when it comes. Will you be ready?"

"Ready to arrest my boss? That fascist prick? I'm ready now."

"Who's going to help you? Is anyone armed?"

"I have a couple of tough boys with me who can keep Brudsky quiet. The challenge will be keeping them from killing him. And then, the cops are on our side."

"How do you know?"

Katerina interrupted. "It's time to meet the deputy commander of police," she said.

The deputy commander of police was the first young man that Maurice met in Kalush. He was tall and thin and his blond hair was cut short like a brush. In short, he looked more like Hitler's Aryan ideal than any German soldier Maurice had ever seen.

He wore civilian clothes to meet Maurice and Katerina on the quay beside the river. "Walter Frankovsk," he said, shaking Maurice's hand.

"You're deputy commander of police?"

He nodded and fell into step beside them. "I joined in 1941, when Bandera told us to." The leader of the Ukrainian Insurgent Army had encouraged Ukrainians to join the German-sponsored police force in occupied Ukraine. When the time came, he would have a cadre of trained, armed men to form the nucleus of a professional army. "I've been here since then, working my way up. But the Germans put that prick Zalushin in charge."

"Will you be ready when I get the signal?" Maurice asked.

"I'll have groups of men where you need them within an hour," he said, his blue eyes flashing. "And Zalushin will be in the ground within five minutes."

Even though he knew the main parts of the plan to take over Kalush were in place, coordinating the plan's execution would require more meetings and discussions. With the Germans and their stooges, not to mention the communist agents, watching everyone and everything, they needed an excuse for gathering. Maurice's solution was setting up Ukrainian cultural organizations. "We need to build the Ukrainian character of Halychyna, so the people identify with Ukraine instead of with Poland or the Soviet Union," he told Katerina. "We need to reinforce the Ukrainian national character."

Through Katerina, Sewchuk and the other main contacts, Maurice worked to convince people. He went from home to home, church to church, hall to hall, convincing the locals to set up Prosvita Ukrainian Reading Societies, Ukrainian Scouting, church auxiliaries, charities for widows and orphans, Ukrainian schools.

The city administrator was dubious about signing the permission for a dance. He was one of the few Ukrainians who had held a civic post under Poland, and the Germans had put him in charge more out of convenience than any confidence in his ability. He had dark brown hair and eyes and a sharp nose. A shapeless, dark brown patch mottled his left cheek, and when Maurice saw similar marks on the Commissar's hands, he knew they were burn scars.

"Ukrainian folk songs?" he said as he read Maurice's application. "We do not want to encourage nationalism."

"This would only be to reinforce the local culture," Maurice said. "To give the people a little celebration after being liberated from the communists by the Third Reich."

"The last thing we need in Kalush is to encourage nationalism," said the administrator. He looked up from the application form. "The countryside is crawling with partisans, communists and nationalists alike."

"I assure you, comrade, the intent is only celebratory. And if people feel happy in their current situation, then they'll feel happy about the general government, too."

The administrator turned to look at the picture of Adolf Hitler on the wall, and considered. "Perhaps you're right. All right, we can try one for now. I'll be watching, though."

The first Friday night dance was held at the newly established Prosvita Ukrainian Reading Society, which set up in a hall that had belonged to a Polish association before 1939. Maurice joined a group of local men and women in the evenings to repair and clean the hall as much as they could, and by Friday night, it looked a little less depressing than it had before. There was no glass to be bought, so they had boarded up broken windows and decorated the insides of the window frames with colourful embroidered cloths.

A small orchestra set up: three old men with battered fiddles, two women who sang and a thirteen-year-old boy who knew a few chords on the bandura. When people began to arrive at around eight o'clock, the band struck up an old Volyn tune.

Not a bad crowd for the first time, Maurice thought. The hall was three-quarters full. A few older men danced with their wives, a group of teenaged girls and young women danced together. There were almost no young men. *How many are still serving in the Red Army, how many are imprisoned by the Germans. How many are dead?* Maurice wondered.

Both the local Catholic and Orthodox priests came. The dancers sat and sipped tea until someone gave the priests a glass of vodka each. The fathers toasted each other, raised their glasses to the band and shot their drinks back simultaneously. The band struck up a lively polka, the young women jumped up to dance and everyone else visibly relaxed.

The city administrator arrived at nine, precisely, with a rifle-bearing guard. He stood in the doorway to survey the crowd. "I know this tune," he said. "It's Russian, isn't it? Not Ukrainian."

"It's universal," Maurice said, pressing a glass of vodka into the administrator's hand. He gave another to the guard, who smiled and downed it immediately.

The administrator looked at each person dancing, sitting, standing or playing in the band. He swallowed his drink and held out the glass. Maurice refilled it.

"It seems all right, Bury," the Commissar said. "Music, food, drinks. The people do seem to be enjoying themselves. Good job."

"Thank you, sir. Will you join us?"

The administrator continued to scan the hall. He sighed. "No, I do not think so. Not this time, anyway. I want a report about the event on my desk tomorrow morning, however: names of everyone who attended, the music played, any other activities. Good night."

He drank his second glass of vodka and left.

When the door closed behind him, Maurice let out the breath he had been holding for longer than could remember. He drank a shot of vodka and went to join the party.

Maurice danced with two mothers who had accompanied their daughters to the dance. Having done his duty, he took Katerina's hand. "Dance with me, pretty lady."

"Oh, Maurice. Don't we have more important things to think about?"

"More important than dancing with a beautiful woman?" he answered, searching her deep blue eyes. "What could be more important than that?"

Maurice and Katerina danced, and Maurice was surprised when he realized he felt happy. In that moment, holding Katerina in his arms and dancing on the uneven floor of the run-down hall, he felt simply happy. He leaned closer and breathed in Katerina's scent, felt her hair against his cheek. He closed his eyes and savoured the feeling of her soft body in his arms.

Then it was time to leave. The band put away their instruments and Maurice and Katerina walked quickly, hand in hand, rushing to get home before they were arrested for being out past the German-enforced curfew.

In the house, Katerina would not let go of Maurice's hand. She led him upstairs and into her bedroom. She finally let him go so that she could light the lamp.

Maurice sat on the edge of the bed and looked into her eyes. In the yellow coal-oil light of the lamp, he could see that those eyes were wide. Not with fear. They shone with a fire, and behind that fire was a cold strength, like steel.

He looked at those eyes for a long moment and then he leaned forward and kissed her. She pressed her mouth into his, wrapped her arms around Maurice's shoulders and pulled him down onto the bed. She rolled until she was on top of him and pulled his shirt until all the buttons popped off. She fell on him then, her kisses hot on his neck and chest. Maurice reached for her, but she sat up quickly and pulled her dress over her head. Maurice slid her brassiere off her shoulders and leaned back a little to admire her.

Naked, she was glorious. Her nipples were deep red in the yellow lamplight, her hair falling golden around her shoulders. She set Maurice on fire. The lamp burned all its coal oil, flickered and died away, leaving them in the dark long before Katerina's fire waned.

Chapter 13:
The Battle of Ternopyl
Kalush, October 1943 – April 1944

Thus began a new pattern for Maurice: he rose early each day to teach in the Ridna Shkola. After work and at dances, concerts and church picnics, he discussed plans with Ukrainian nationalists. At night, he prepared lessons and marked tests—and coded and decoded messages for UPA.

Maurice often had difficulty believing the coded messages he still received and forwarded to the UPA network. He would spend hours, carefully checking his decoding before compiling them, coding his report and burning the originals.

Soviets capture Kharkiv

Germans evacuate Belgorod, Red Army takes it.

The Red Army was coming closer.

The UPA now found itself fighting a multi-sided war. While most of the operations of small groups of men and women aimed to disrupt the Germans and liberate confiscated food and supplies, larger units skirmished with units of the Polish Home Army, which itself was fighting an underground struggle against the

Germans and anticipating the arrival of the Red Army. Maurice felt sick to his stomach when he read or heard about units of the UPA attacking Poles in their homes and forcing them out of what it considered Ukrainian territory, and when he read about Polish Home Army reprisals.

It was another war, obscured by the titanic struggle between Germany and Russia.

By the end of 1943, the Red Army had pushed the Germans out of eastern Ukraine all the way back to the Dnipro River. A savage battle for the Ukrainian capital of Kyiv, the USSR's third-largest city, began with a Soviet bombardment on November 3. It took the Red Army more than a month of intensive, destructive fighting to take the city and gain the western bank of the Dnipro River. Then on December 24, they began their Winter Offensive and drove the Germans to the 1939 Polish border by January 3, 1944.

In March, 1944, the Soviets began what they came to call their "mud offensive." The coded messages described how, within two weeks, the Red Army had swept from the Dnipro to the Dniester Rivers, hundreds of kilometres away, encircling hundreds of thousands of German soldiers and whole divisions. Maurice remembered the last messages from operatives in the east in March: the Red Army was moving with astonishing speed, shattering the Germans. Then they crossed the Dniester, capturing the territory they had lost almost as fast as the Germans had conquered it in 1941.

Maurice returned to the empty apartment almost daily and found more messages to compile and send on.

13 March: Panzers attack south-east of Ternopyl. Red Army pushed back.

21 March: Red Army encircles 200,000 Germans southwest of Vinnitsya.

Then the messages from the east ceased.

From the west, he read one that sent a chill through his body: "Hitler has declared Ternopyl a fortified city. Ordered Germans to defend to the last round fired."

The village of Nastaciv, where his mother and sister were, was only twenty kilometres south.

In March 1944, two Red Army fronts, in total 16 complete armies, approached Ternopyl from the east and south-east. Ternopyl was a critical point on the railway in Ukraine, and losing it meant the Germans would have a longer supply route for its forces still in Ukraine.

Civilians evacuated the city, running to the west as the 4,600-man German garrison dug in. They were low on ammunition but had plenty of food and other supplies, and orders not to surrender.

The Red Army began with a massive bombardment by heavy artillery and the air, which lasted for days. The Germans fought back, repelled tanks and infantry from the city's streets several times, as the commander, Generalmajor von Neindorff, repeatedly radioed Berlin for permission to withdraw. Berlin repeated its order to stay until the last round was fired.

By the end of March, the Red Army had surrounded Ternopyl, keeping up the pressure of bombardment and attacks by mortars, tanks and infantry. Units of the German garrison tried again and again to break out to the west, while other German armies from Poland made repeated attempts to relieve their comrades. They all failed.

On April 15, the few remaining Germans tried one more time to escape the cauldron. A few made it, but Generalmajor von Neindorff was killed in the attempt. By this time, the Germans had a quarter of their men left squeezed into a residential part of the city. Waves of bombing and strafing did not let up.

The battle raged for three weeks. Out of 4,500 men, 45 German soldiers, none of them officers, managed to escape. The city of Ternopyl itself was destroyed. A tenth of the houses remained standing.

Now the front lines between Germany and Russia separated Maurice from his family.

Chapter 14: Changing occupiers

Kalush, July 1944

Sleep eluded Maurice and Katerina on a humid summer night. They lay on top of the bed covers, under an open window, hoping for a breeze that never came.

Then a blast shook the house, rattling the windows. Maurice felt the bed move across the floor and heard glass breaking as a picture fell off its hook on the wall.

He pulled the curtain aside to see a red glow at the edge of town, illuminating black clouds billowing into the predawn sky. As he watched, another explosion beyond the fire shook the house again.

"What is it?" Katerina asked. "An air raid?"

"I don't know," Maurice said. "I don't hear airplanes." He pulled pants and a shirt over his pajamas and ran downstairs, listening for planes, tanks, anything. He pulled on a coat and his boots and paused at the door. Still no sound of airplanes, but he thought he could hear a train in the distance, and somewhere, shouts of frightened people. But no sirens.

Firelight reflected off the heavy clouds. The eerie glow was bright enough for him to find his way through the blacked-out streets. The smell of burning oil and wood got stronger as he followed the flickering light, and he could hear the flames over the shouts of a crowd.

It was the train station that burned, and Maurice did not see any sign of the fire department. Then he remembered that the Germans had taken the trucks two months earlier for their own use. Maurice pushed through the crowd until he could see that the main building was engulfed in flames so intense, he felt as if his skin was drying and tightening around the corners of his mouth. He could also see that the tracks in both directions had been blown up, with a series of craters stretching as far as he could see.

He turned and followed another flickering glow to the armoury, which had housed the German force in Kalush. It had already burned to the ground.

Beyond the train station, an oil depot was also aflame, along with a food warehouse and several houses. The inhabitants stood outside, weeping. "Scorched earth," said another spectator beside Maurice.

Maurice turned. "What?"

"Scorched earth," the man repeated. "The Germans are retreating, and they're leaving nothing behind for the Russians to use. It's the same thing the Russians did three years ago."

"Except the Red Army never burned down people's houses. That was Germans then, too," Maurice answered, and knew he had said too much. He turned and walked away from the stranger as quickly as he could.

He pushed past crowds of people as mystified by the events as he was, reaching the central square again just as the sunrise turned the sky yellow and pink, and he had to stop. Men and women in ill-fitting uniforms ran into the square. Some carried old rifles, others handguns. A few wore steel helmets. He saw two men batter the city hall's front doors open with their rifle butts.

An officer on a proud stallion rode into the square. "Attention, citizens! Kalush is now under the control of the *Armia Krajowa*, the Polish Home Army. The Germans have withdrawn and we will administer all civic functions until the re-establishment of the free Polish state."

Where did they come from? Maurice wondered. The communists exiled almost all the Poles to Siberia in 1940. Apparently, a few had remained and contacted the AK.

Men and women crowded closer, asking questions, but the officer ignored them. He nudged the horse closer to the city hall and shouted orders.

More AK soldiers, men and women, appeared in the square. The officer on the horse pointed and spoke loudly, ordering them to tasks. Maurice hurried home.

The Polish Home Army's reign was brief. The next day, the Red Army paraded into the central square as heavy planes roared overhead, streaking west to bomb the Germans where they tried to firm up their defences. Maurice could hear the explosions, miles away.

Katerina came home late in the evening, her face grim. "The NKVD have arrested anyone in a Polish Home Army uniform, along with anyone they suspected of membership," she said. Maurice poured her a glass of vodka. "The girl who works in the town hall told me she heard them offering the Poles a choice: join the Red Army, or visit Siberia permanently."

"Have they said anything about Ukrainians?" Maurice asked.

Katerina shook her head. "Nothing that she heard. I didn't hear anything, either." She tossed her vodka back.

"If UPA is going to make a move, it's going to have to be soon," Maurice said.

The next morning, July 28, Maurice and Katerina again woke to explosions in the predawn dark. Maurice chanced a look out the window. Along with continuing explosions from the west, he heard the familiar buzzing roar of German dive-bombers and fighter planes.

"The Germans are counter-attacking," he said, turning away from the window.

"To the cellar," Katerina said, urgently, pulling a coat over her nightdress as she walked out of the bedroom.

Maurice again pulled his pants on over his pajamas and followed her downstairs. As they went outside to the root cellar's entrance at the back of the house, they saw the next-door neighbours, a family with two small daughters, coming into their yard. "Can we stay with you?" said the mother, a thin woman with dark hair and perpetual dark circles under her eyes. Maurice remembered that her name was Krystyna, and thought her husband was Pavlo, but he could not remember their last name.

They heard three more explosions rolling over the roofs of the houses. The little girls flinched. They were both thin with long, straight hair, and both wore thin jackets over nightdresses. The smaller one, whom Maurice estimated was eight years old, clutched her mother's waist.

Katerina nodded and Maurice pulled open the doors to the cellar, set at an angle on the ground. He stood aside to allow Katerina and the neighbour family to precede him. Katerina turned on the single, dim bulb in the cellar, which hung from a rafter at the end of a single wire that snaked up the staircase, through a hole drilled through the door frame. The cellar smelled of damp earth, garlic and apples.

The two little girls sat on a wooden case against the back wall of the cellar. Their mother crouched between them, arms over their shoulders. "Don't cry," she said. "We're safe here."

"Thank you," Pavlo said to Maurice. A shell exploded somewhere close enough that dust fell from the ceiling of the cellar. The younger girl began to sob.

On shelves along the length of the cellar, Maurice and Katerina had stored food over the months: jars of pickled beets and cucumbers, potatoes, cheese, dry bread cut into slices, sausages that could last a long time in the cool darkness, a barrel of rain water. And a few bottles of vodka.

Katerina cut two pieces of cheese and poured cups of water for the girls. Distracted by the food, the girls stopped crying, even when another explosion shook the cellar. They waited without speaking, listening to explosions seeming to approach, then recede.

After an hour, the sound of gunfire replaced the explosions. It got closer until they heard rumbling that Maurice knew was the sound of panzers and trucks. Then shouting, more gunfire, and the trucks receded.

By mid-afternoon, they heard only silence. The air in the cellar was stuffy and warm. Maurice lifted one cellar door a little, relishing the feeling of fresh air on his face as he peeked out into the back garden. There was nothing to see but the garden, trees and a beautiful blue sky. He thought he could hear trucks and tanks a few blocks away, but he could not be certain.

"I think the fighting's stopped," he said to the people in the cellar. "Stay here and I'll see what I can." He lowered the door slowly so as to make no sound, and then crept around the house, keeping his body close to the ground.

The street in front of the house was deserted. He walked slowly, silently to the curb and looked down to the larger avenue at the end of the block, just in time to see a German half-track rumble by, followed by jogging soldiers carrying submachine guns.

Grey uniforms. Germans.

The Germans held the city for a day. Maurice, Katerina and their neighbours, like most of the citizens of the town, hid in their basements and cellars again as the Red Army blasted its way back in. The fighting retreated to the west, leaving the small city blackened and battered.

Chapter 15:
The plot foiled

Kalush, August 1944

A few evenings later, grey clouds hung low and the air was heavy with water. Thunder growled somewhere, but the rain stubbornly refused to give Kalush relief from the heat. Maurice found a tattered, dirty slip of paper at the drop-off. He went home as quickly as he could without appearing to be rushing.

In his room, he pulled the blind closed before turning the coal-oil lamp brighter, then unfolded the tattered slip of paper. He sat down and began decoding. Every letter he translated filled him simultaneously with more excitement and dread.

"Begin eight-eight."

On August 8, just a week away, UPA was going to move against the Soviet occupiers. UPA's commanders apparently theorized that the Red Army would be busy against the Germans, and the Poles had been eliminated as a threat in this corner of the country. Uprisings would happen in other cities at the same time, but Maurice could not know the details. All he did know what that his people had to take charge in Kalush: the police force, the railroad station, waterworks, electrical supply, armoury.

Apparently, his commanders did not know the Germans had destroyed the train station and the armoury. Even so, taking over the town would be risky. Maurice knew men would die. Maybe he would.

He went to the bedroom, where Katerina had already gone to bed. "Spread the word starting tomorrow," he said. "At dawn, August 8, we start."

He heard movement, and then Katerina lit her lamp and adjusted it so that he could just see the delicate triangle of her face. Her hair was tied back for sleep. A few blond strands escaped, curling around the gentle curve of her cheeks. She wore a plain nightgown, open at the throat, but sleeveless. He could not take his eyes from the curve where her shoulder became her slender neck.

He swallowed. "Tell only the key people, so that they can make sure they're ready to move the day before. Need to know only. We can't let word spread too far, but we have to be absolutely ready."

"I know, Maurice. You don't have to tell me." Her voice was low and calm.

These children's concerts are tedious, Maurice admitted to himself.

He had lost count of the number of times he had sat in the once-Polish, now-Ukrainian hall to listen to a mediocre band play. Tonight, he endured the church children's choir torture his ears with "Mama Sewed a Kerchief."

He nodded and smiled at the local ladies, nodded at the local notables like the school headmaster and the Catholic priest. A lady who wanted to be known as prominent in the town talked to him for a while about raising the children's spirits after the fighting, and he pretended to listen. He could not concentrate on the concert, though. The uprising was to start in three days. Plans and contingencies swirled through his mind.

The children's choir left the stage. Six women from the Catholic Church choir took the stage and sang "Marichka." When they finished, a teenaged boy leaped onto the stage.

He startled everyone because he wore traditional Cossack garb: baggy red pants, tall red boots and a white, collarless shirt embroidered at the neck. He had even shaved his head except for a single long, black tassel of hair, tied together, Cossack style.

"Brothers!" he shouted, and every conversation in the hall stopped. He took a breath and began declaiming, as loudly as he could, "Ukraine Awake," by Taras Shevchenko, the nineteenth-century nationalist Ukrainian poet.

Oh, no. Not today. Not with the communists arresting everyone who looks at them funny.

The boy had not reached the end of the first stanza when a cry from the door made everyone freeze: "ENOUGH."

At the door, hands behind his back, stood a commissar, a political officer in his distinctive red-patched uniform. Twelve NKVD soldiers, rifles in hand, fanned across the hall. Two jumped onto the stage and dragged the Cossack boy off with them.

Women cried out. Men protested until NKVD rifle butts bashed in their teeth.

The commissar stepped onto the stage. "This recital is politically incorrect, contravening the spirit of the Revolution. Nationalistic expressions will not be tolerated," he said. The soldiers grabbed the orchestra and pulled them one by one out the front door.

Maurice dashed through a side door. The hall was just off the main square, and he could hear heavy vehicles rumbling and grinding along the darkening streets. The sun had just set, leaving the sky a dusky purple.

Katerina.

He ran for the square. In it were four big trucks of a model he had never seen before. In Roman letters, he made out a brand name: Studebaker.

What the hell is a Studebaker?

Red Army soldiers leaped out of the trucks, submachine guns at the ready. Maurice could see red stripes and triangles on their uniforms: NKVD. Stalin's security police, the enforcers of Communist orthodoxy.

Shots rang out of the police station that faced onto the square and one of NKVD men fell. The rest crouched or took cover behind their trucks and anything else they could find and as a man, fired on the station. Maurice found his feet and dashed behind the corner of the hall.

The firing stopped and the sergeant of the NKVD entered the police station, followed by four men. Maurice heard more gunshots from inside the station, and after a minute, the NKVD men returned, dragging the blond deputy, Walter Frankovsk, by the arms.

They threw him on the ground and he sprang up immediately, shouting. With the uproar from the hall and the square all around, Maurice could not hear what he said, but his meaning was clear: "Ukrainians! It's time to rise up!"

It's not. Not yet. UPA is not ready. Not for three more days.

The police commander came out of the station then, a blunt-faced Russian with a scar across his forehead. He buckled his gun-belt and smoothed his uniform. He stopped in front of Frankovsk, who stopped yelling to glare at his commander.

The commander calmly looked at the young man for a long moment, and then in one smooth movement, drew his sidearm and fired it into Frankovsk's forehead.

Maurice turned and ran down the street, ignoring the uproar behind him. *Katerina* was all he could think.

He found her in her bedroom, throwing clothes and other things into a soft bag. "Never mind that," he said. "Let's go."

"Someone talked," she said, abandoning the bag. "Fucking Ivan has arrested all our people."

Maurice grabbed her hand and pulled her down the stairs and out the back door, stopping only long enough for him to take his gun, the liberated Luger, from its hiding place. They slipped through the back gate and ran down an alley toward the river.

"Where are we going?" Katerina panted.

"Anywhere. Out of the city." He saw the quay ahead, but then saw another one of those Studebaker trucks grinding down the quay, its headlights bouncing as the wheels hit potholes. He pulled Katerina close and felt her body press against his.

"This way," she said, taking his hand this time and leading him into a dark street. From the square, they heard screams and gunshots. A submachine gun chattered, followed by more screams.

They stopped at a stable. "Kick in the door," Katerina told him. Maurice raised a foot and kicked with the sole of his foot beside the latch. Wood splintered and the door shook, then swung slightly toward them.

They slipped into the smell of hay and horse and manure. A horse grunted and shuffled in its stall. As his eyes adjusted to the darkness, Maurice could make out a small horse, nervous at the presence of strangers. Behind it were a small buggy and tack.

He took the bridle, but when he tried to slip it over the horse's head, it reared and whinnied. He tried to quiet it and managed to put the bridle on, but it neighed again.

"Let me," said Katerina. "You put on its saddle."

Maurice fumbled in the dark and managed to get the saddle on the horse. As he tightened the cinch, Katerina murmured softly to the horse, calming it.

They saw a light through the spaces between the boards that made up the barn's walls. "The owner is coming!" Katerina hissed. Maurice swung onto the horse but before he could tell Katerina to open the door, it slid open. They could see a man silhouetted in the opening, holding a lantern aloft. "Who's there?" he demanded.

Maurice slapped the reins with one hand and reached for Katerina with the other. The horse reared, neighed and bolted. Maurice pulled Katerina up onto the horse's back as it flew out of the stable. The man with the lantern fell to the ground, yelling, but they were away.

"Turn right here!" Katerina said at the first corner, her arms wrapped tight around his waist. Maurice thought it was the wrong way, back toward the square, but he complied. "Now left," she said.

They zigzagged their way out of the city. Every time the horse veered around a corner, Maurice felt he was about to fall off. Katerina's grip tightened until he could hardly breathe. Just when he thought they were getting close to the edge of the city and safety, two lights flared in of them. "Halt!" called a voice, and Maurice could see soldiers silhouetted in the headlights.

He pulled in the reins, thinking furiously of a story to tell the NKVD. But Katerina reached around him and pulled the reins. The horse veered right into another dark lane.

A submachine gun chattered behind them. The horse screamed and fell to the side, spilling Maurice and Katerina onto soft grass.

He struggled to his knees. In the darkness, he could just make out Katerina, sprawled in a narrow alley. Crouching, he touched her shoulder. Her arm flopped onto the ground and he felt a warm, sticky wetness on his hand.

"Katerina?" he whispered. "Katerina?"

At the end of the alley, he heard soldiers coming closer. "Come out with your hands up!" someone called.

Maurice straightened Katerina's limbs as gently as he could. Then he crawled backwards, keeping the fallen horse between himself and the soldiers. He found a bush and crawled behind it, flattening himself onto the ground.

Two soldiers stepped closer, cautiously. The horse whinnied and kicked, but could not get up.

"Who's there?" said one soldier.

The other stepped up to Katerina's body and touched her arm with his boot. "A woman. She's dead."

"Is she alone?"

The soldier scanned the ground as best he could in the dark. "I think so."

The horse whinnied again, a pitiful sound. It struggled but could not rise. The second soldier stepped over and shot it once in the head.

Maurice pushed himself backward along the ground, away from the soldiers, careful not to make the slightest sound. An officer came around the buggy then, shining an electric torch around. "It is just the one rider?" he said.

"Yes, comrade lieutenant. A woman."

The lieutenant shone his torch around again, and Maurice thrust his face into the dirt. He held his breath until he heard the officer say "All right. Take her body back to the square."

Maurice continued to push himself backward until his feet hit something solid: a house or an outbuilding. In the dark, he couldn't tell which, but he felt around with his feet until he found a corner and pushed himself back around it. Pressing his back against the wall, he stood.

"What was that?" the lieutenant said. He shone his light to the side of the building where Maurice had lain a moment before.

"I didn't hear anything, Lieutenant," said the first soldier.

"You two go check."

Maurice heard the soldiers stepping cautiously toward him. He slid along the wall, as quietly he could until he reached the far corner. He found himself in the front garden of a modest house. Beyond a low hedge was a dark street. He dashed across the garden and jumped the hedge, then crouched and ran as fast as he could.

"Over there!" said one of the soldiers. He could hear them stomping toward him. He ran faster still, not worrying about staying low. At the first corner, he turned and then jumped into the next yard. He crossed it, scaled a fence and ran across another garden. Three fences and gardens later, he found a dark alley. At one end, he could see the lights of a truck and silhouettes of soldiers. He turned and ran silently the other way.

An hour later, he passed beyond the limits of the city of Kalush. He guessed at north-east from the moon and figuring that downhill from the Carpathian foothills around Kalush was roughly the right direction. He thought going downhill would be easier, but in the dark he stumbled often. Downhill was harder on his knees than he expected. He looked up toward the crescent moon as if it could tell him something, and his toe hit a rock or rise in the ground. He pitched forward and scraped his hand, biting back a curse in case Soviet soldiers were close enough to hear.

The rushing, burbling sound of a mountain stream came from his left. He stood, testing his step to make sure he hadn't twisted his ankles, but the only place that hurt was the heel of his left hand where he had scraped it. He held it to his mouth and tasted blood. *Mine or Katerina's?*

Carefully, he stepped toward the sound of water, walking around bushes and down a slippery, grassy slope. Then he could see movement under the starlight: a narrow brook, bubbling and frothing. He knelt at the bank and dipped his left hand in, then jerked it out again—it was so cold, his skin felt like it was burning. He clenched his jaw and thrust his hand in to the wrist, and held it there as he imagined the icy, swirling water washing off the blood and dirt. When his hand was numb, he pulled it out and flexed the fingers, wincing at the pain of the cuts and the cold. He pulled his sleeve down over it to try to dry and warm it, but that did not make much difference.

He continued downhill, walking as steadily as he could. He found a road that he thought led north-east, toward Ternopyl. *I have to report that the plan is gone. How far did the leak spread? How much do the Communists know about the UPA uprising? I have to report in.*

Now that the Red Army had taken Kalush, the front no longer separated him from his family. But Ternopyl was still a hundred kilometres away, his mother's home in Nastaciv not much closer. He needed help now.

He followed a track across the fields until he found another dirt road, turning toward a small town he knew called Bil'shivtsi. He had a UPA contact there, a man named Romanenko. *I'll ask him for help to get home. A horse, a wagon. Anything he can spare.*

Chapter 16: Nightmare journey

Between Kalush and Ternopyl, August 1944

When the sky in the east began to gray, Maurice looked for shelter; a place to hide from the Soviets during the daylight hours. He found a stand of trees near the road and pulled down evergreen boughs to make bed and covers. As the sun rose, he settled into it, pulling boughs over his head.

He tried not to think about how hungry and thirsty he felt. Only when he felt well-hidden, did he let himself weep for Katerina. And when his tears dried, he thought of the others, the dedicated Ukrainians arrested by the NKVD. Frankovsk, executed in the square in front of everyone.

Voices woke him. The sun was high, filtering through the branches over him. He raised his head slowly, moving the branches covering him until he could see who was speaking. A group of men stood in the road: seven wearing the brown uniforms of the Red Army, submachine guns ready, and a man in civilian clothes and a belt around his jacket, a tattered peaked cap on his head and a pistol in his hand facing them. "Comrades," said the single man, in Russian. "I am so happy to see you!" He had a Muscovite accent, Maurice thought.

"And who are you?" said the corporal, the ranking soldier in the uniformed group. "Comrades!" said the solitary man. "I am a partisan."

"Partisan?" the corporal repeated.

"I have been fighting for the people of the motherland these past months," said the civilian. "I am with the UHA." That was the communist Ukrainian partisan group operating behind the German lines since 1941.

The corporal raised his gun and fired once. The partisan dropped like a sack of flour. One of the soldiers dropped his submachine gun on the ground.

"Don't trust people you find in the country," the corporal said.

"Comrade, he said he was one of us," said one of the soldiers.

The corporal punched him in the nose, and the soldier dropped to his knees, howling. "Look at his boots, you idiot," said the corporal. "This man was a German escapee. Maybe a deserter. Probably. I don't know. But you can't turn your back on these people. Half of this country is under UPA. Traitors. Nazis themselves. They'll kill you the first chance they get. Did he put down his gun? No. Don't trust anyone you meet out here."

One of the soldiers helped the man who'd been hit to get up. The corporal shouldered his rifle and the troop marched down the road. That was when Maurice noticed that his hands were trembling.

Much, much too close.

When the Soviet soldiers were out of sight, Maurice followed a track across the fields until he found another dirt road that he recognized as leading to Bil'shivtsi.

The wind had shifted, blowing from the north, cooling the afternoon. Maurice wiped sweat off his forehead. He felt empty. His feet and his back ached, and his shoes were wet. He could feel the old wound in his leg hurting again.

I need rest and safety. And food. I need food. He tried to hurry, but he had to pause often, ducking behind trees along the road whenever he saw someone else, in case they were the Red Army or some local official.

His head felt like his brain was pushing his eyes out of their sockets when he reached the village of Bil'shivtsi in the mid-afternoon. The town nestled in a valley between low hills. He saw only one other man as he walked through the village, who moved quickly without looking up. Everyone else was staying indoors, away from the armies that had passed through it.

Romanenko lived on a farm at the edge of the village, and Maurice, feeling like he was walking through mud, went around the brown brick house to the back door. After climbing one wooden step, he felt like he didn't have the strength to even knock on the door. Somehow, he managed it, and then held his head in his hands to try to relieve some of the pounding pressure.

Finally, the door opened. A small, young woman with large brown eyes stood there, wearing an old dress and an apron. She had light brown hair that hung to her shoulders. If he weren't so exhausted, Maurice would have appreciated her beauty.

"Well?" she demanded, and Maurice realized he was just staring at her. He could not think of what to say. "What do you want? Are you crazy?"

"Romanenko," he croaked, his throat was so dry it felt like he had swallowed sand. He started to stumble back and nearly fell off the back step, but the woman caught his arm.

"Yes, this is Romanenko's. I am Maria Romanenka. Who are you and what do you want?"

"UPA," was all he could say. Fear sprang onto Maria's face. She looked past his shoulder and all around as she pulled him inside, shutting the door quietly.

"My husband is not home," she said, as Maurice fell onto a kitchen chair.

The air in the house felt cooler than outside. "Water," Maurice said. She poured a mug from a large jug and Maurice gulped it down at once. He felt relief wash through him and his head began to droop toward the table top. Maria put a kettle on the pietsch and cut a thick slice of bread from a home-made loaf. She put it on a plate in front of him, with butter, and disappeared into another room.

She returned with a bundle of cloth and a basin of water. "Your clothes are filthy and smelly. Change into these." She left again, and Maurice rose clumsily. His fingers felt as sensitive as sausages as he undid his buttons. It seemed to take forever, but he managed to strip, wash his body with a cloth, dry himself and pull on underwear, socks and pants before Maria returned to the kettle's whistle. She set a cup of tea in front of Maurice as he pulled on Romanenko's shirt and then a jacket. She tossed his clothes into a basket on the floor and put his wet shoes on top of the pietsch to dry.

Romanenko was shorter than Maurice, and there was a gap between the hems of the pants and the top of the socks. The shirt cuffs came halfway down his forearms.

His noticed his hands were shaking as he picked up the mug. He made an effort to control it, enough at least so he could drink the tea without slopping it onto his hand.

The heat of the tea burned down his throat, but he swallowed greedily. The pain in his head decreased a little.

Maria sat and watched him until he had eaten the bread and drunk half the tea. "Who are you?"

Maurice looked her in the eyes and said "Zorenko."

"You're taking foolish chances using words like that. You've never seen me before."

"I had no choice. I need help. I need to get back to Ternopyl. UPA is finished in Kalush."

"You talk too much. How do you know I won't report you to the NKVD?"

"You're Romanenko's wife."

"How do you know I didn't kick the bastard out the door and turn to Russia?"

"You gave me clean clothes, food and tea. Why else would you do that?" He tried to smile, and surprised himself when he succeeded. He relaxed a little more and took his first good look at the house.

It was much the same as every other farmhouse in western Ukraine, built around the stone oven and furnace. It was whitewashed the same colour as the walls. Embroidered curtains framed windows that looked out to the fields, turning gold by the low sun.

"Where is Petro?" Maurice asked.

The rumble of trucks interrupted Maria. Frowning, she stood and went around the pietsch to the front room of the house. Maurice followed, hanging back as she went to the front window. Still, he could see those damned Studebakers proceeding along the muddy road to the centre of the village. It's the NKVD, he knew. They're here to round up the resistance, make sure there are no Germans hiding in attics or outbuildings, no UPA officers.

Before they could say another word, something bashed on the front door, hard. "Open up!" a harsh voice yelled. Maria screamed, her hand in front of her mouth. The door bashed again and Maurice stepped behind the pietsch just as it swung open.

"What do you want?" he heard Maria demand, breathless with fear, as booted feet stepped inside the house.

There was a pause and Maurice worried the soldiers at the door would hear his hammering heart. Then he heard a voice, a young man, laughing. He heard the NKVD soldier take a step and say "Harna jinka" — "pretty lady."

Maurice stepped around the pietsch to see a lone soldier, rifle held loosely in one hand, holding Maria's chin in his other. He was young, with brown hair peeking out from under his helmet.

"That's my wife you're pawing," he said, hoping he sounded sterner than he felt.

The soldier let Maria go and spun toward Maurice, hefting his rifle clumsily. Maurice could have shot the soldier easily. He'd better smarten up soon, or he'll be dead.

"Why were you hiding?" the soldier demanded. He had the round face and large brown eyes Maurice associated with Russians.

"I wasn't hiding, comrade," Maurice said. "I was drinking tea." He stepped to Maria and put his arm around her shoulder. "Did he hurt you, dear?"

Maria looked at him, eyes wide, mouth gaping. She looked at the soldier, then back at Maurice, seeming to struggle to find an answer. After a long moment, she shook her head.

Maurice turned to the soldier. "Shouldn't you be looking for the enemy instead of bothering poor farmers' wives?"

"I am looking for the enemy, comrade," said the soldier. He lowered his rifle a little. Stupid man, Maurice thought.

"Well, go ahead and look," Maurice said. hoping that Petro Romanenko hadn't been stupid enough to leave anything incriminating around the farm. The soldier scowled, and keeping his rifle pointed approximately in Maurice's direction, strode to the back of the house and looked behind the pietsch. He moved toward the single bedroom and looked inside it, too. Giving Maurice one last scowl, he stepped out the open door and whistled through his teeth. Maurice saw two other soldiers returning from Romanenko's barn. The soldier on front step raised his chin quizzically. One of the others shook his head. Without another word or backward glance, they moved to the next farm.

Maurice stood still, one arm around Maria's shoulders. She was shaking. He waited until the soldiers were out of sight, then released Maria and shut the door. His hands were shaking. "Where is Petro?"

Maria sat on a wooden chair. "I don't know. He has not been home for four days. I think he's either dead, or taken prisoner by the NKVD."

Maurice looked out the window. Evening was beginning to turn the grey sky to black. "Do you still have a horse and wagon?" Maria nodded. "Pack up a few things. You're coming with me."

"Where?"

"Nastaciv. It's near Ternopyl."

"Why?"

"Because it's my home, and the Germans are determined to hold onto Ternopyl."

"But that's farther east. It's deeper in Soviet territory, now."

"There's no way for you to get behind the German lines. Do you really want to?"

Maria shook her head, eyes on the floor.

"I need to find out whether my family is still alive. And if the communists have your husband in custody, they're going to come for you soon, despite what that idiotic soldier thinks. You're not safe here. You pack, and I'll get the wagon ready. We'll leave as soon as it's dark."

He went to the back door before Maria could argue any more. His boots sat on the pietsch, but they were still damp. He tied the laces together, then slung them over his shoulder. He found a spare pair of old leather boots of Petro's and squeezed his feet into them. They hurt, but they would have to do for a little while.

Exhaustion forgotten, heart pounding with adrenalin, Maurice jogged across the muddy yard to the barn, where he found a single old horse sleeping in a stall next to a cow and a calf. He took the horse out, put on its yoke and hitched it to Romanenko's battered four-wheel wagon. He found a feed bag, a small barrel of horse feed and a coil of rope and threw them into the back, along with a spade and a few other tools. The last thing he did was leave the gate to the cows' stall and the back door open. No need to let a good milk cow starve to death.

It was nearly dark by the time he returned to the house. Maria was in the kitchen, packing bread, cheese and a jar of jam into a basket. A battered cardboard suitcase sat on the floor beside the door.

It took three nights of travel, two days of hiding in groves and sleeping in the back of the wagon, to reach the small river that was the last barrier between Maurice and his mother's farm. The third night was deep, moonless and dark when Maurice and Maria Romanenka reached the outskirts of Nastasiv. Ternopyl lay another 20 kilometres northeast.

Maurice could hardly breathe as the buggy crossed the little bridge over the Nishla River, and then he turned onto the road that led to his mother's home. In the dark, he could not see any damage, any sign that of fighting in the area, but he did not dare to hope until he saw his mother's house in the gloom.

He exhaled, feeling his shoulders droop. Nothing. No damage.

They're all right.

Chapter 17: The Red Army

Nastaciv, August 1944

"The fighting went on for weeks," said Hanna, Maurice's sister, the day after Maurice and Maria arrived at the Kuritsa house in Nastasiv. The four of them, Hanna, Tekla, Maurice and Maria Romanenka sat at the kitchen table next to the pietcsh. "There was a dark cloud over Ternopyl the whole time, reflecting the fires. We could hear the explosions, on and on, day and night. The Russians never let up the whole time. I can't understand how the Germans hung on as long as they did." Tekla nodded. Maria sat quiet, tears in her brown eyes. Maurice knew she was thinking of her husband.

Tekla poured more vodka. "They destroyed the whole city. Completely destroyed. There's not a building standing. The Russians came from all sides. Every day, they bombed the city, from cannons and planes, too. Dropping, dropping, dropping bombs."

"And no soldiers came here? To Nastaciv?" Maurice asked. It's too good to be true.

"The Red Army came close, a few kilometres north. They came through Ostriv," Hanna said. "And the

Germans tried to send reinforcements through Khodachkiv, but the Reds stopped them at Pochapyntsi."

"That's still very close," said Maurice. He sipped his vodka.

All we could hear were the explosions, day after day, all day long," Tekla said. "The cows would not give milk, the chickens stopped laying. We didn't dare go far from the house."

"I'm sorry that I was not here," Maurice said.

"Pff!" Tekla dismissed the idea with a wave of her hand and tossed back a shot of vodka. "There is nothing you could have done. We weren't afraid here—the fighting was all in Ternopyl, twenty kilometres away. It was bad for the animals, but not for us. Still, I'm going to miss the Germans. They bought a lot of vodka."

"The Russians will buy, too, Mama," Hanna said.

"I don't know. The Communists are opposed to commerce," Maurice said.

Tekla smiled. "Communists or not, they like to drink vodka."

The next morning, Maurice stepped outside onto his mother's front doorstep. He lit a cigarette, drew a lungful and turned his face upward. He closed his eyes to exhale and savoured the feeling of the sun on his face. It felt like the first day of peace after his nightmarish journey from Kalush.

We have to find somewhere else for Maria to stay. People will notice two extra residents in this house, and we don't want anyone to ask questions.

The air smelled sweet with hay and growing sugar beets. He looked out at his mother's fields. *They're doing well*, he thought. *We'll have a good crop this year.* He crouched, digging his fingers into the rich black soil. He pulled a few weeds out from between the beets.

He stood again, leaned against the fence and closed his eyes. How much longer will this war last? *Germany lost the war in 1941, when they stopped outside Moscow and Leningrad. Now they're gone. And now, Ukraine has to fight Stalin's USSR to be free.*

The Soviets had pushed the Germans out of almost all Ukraine by the end of spring. In June 1944, they had launched Operation Bagration, which had swept the Germans out of Belarus and pushed them away from Leningrad. By August, the Red Army was on the Vistula River in Poland, and the Polish Home Army was fighting the Germans to control Warsaw. Meanwhile, the Americans, British, Free French and Canadians were penetrating deep into German-occupied France. *Germany won't just surrender, though. Hitler is too stubborn.*

Maurice wondered about Ukraine's chances of independence from the USSR. It would be a political question, he knew, dependent on the will of the countries of the West.

And Poland. A free Poland will claim western Ukraine, Russia the east.

Maybe I should go back to Canada when this is over.

Something clamped his left arm, and then something else grabbed his right. He looked up and felt cold terror when he saw the red stripes on the uniforms on the men holding him by the arms: NKVD, Stalin's political police.

"Come with us, comrade," said one as they pulled him toward a covered truck. They threw him in the back, where a handful of other fearful-looking young men sat on the floor under the watch of another soldier with a machine-gun ready. The engine roared and the truck lurched. One of the young men fell face-down as the truck jolted along.

Maurice knew what this was about. The Red Army needed more men to make up some of the incredible losses of men its victories brought.

At the Nastasiv town hall, the soldiers pushed the young captives into a hall where NKVD soldiers lined all the walls. Slawka, the mayor's daughter whom he had tutored before the war, sat at the reception desk. She watched them come in with wide eyes and open mouth.

Behind a long table, under a huge portrait of Stalin, sat a commissar. Soldiers brought their captives up to him one by one. He took their names and nodded, and soldiers led each one out to another truck to take them to a training camp.

It was Maurice's turn. The commissar looked at him carefully. "How old are you?"

There was no point in lying. "Twenty-five."

"Why aren't you in the army, then, comrade?"

Maurice could not tell them that he already had been in the army, had been captured and then escaped. Explaining that would lead to summary execution for desertion. "I am a teacher in a rural school, exempt from compulsory service."

"Not during wartime," said the captain.

"I am also working on my mother's farm. I'm the only man in the family."

"I think you're a deserter," said the Commissar.

Behind him, Maurice heard Slawka gasp. "Maurice!" she whispered, and he heard her running away.

"No, comrade commissar!" Maurice protested. "No, I was never called up before the Germans invaded, and after that it was too late—"

"You're lying," said the commissar. He only had to look at the NKVD soldiers, and they took Maurice's arms again.

He heard a clatter and then Slawka ran back into the hall with a short, bald man dressed in a rumpled grey suit and tie: her father, Stepan Husar, the mayor. "Please, help him!" said Slawka.

"What's wrong, Comrade Commissar?" asked the mayor, a little out of breath.

"Nothing you need concern yourself with, Comrade," the Commissar sneered. "This is an Army matter."

"But why have you arrested this man?" Husar's hair was messed and his tie was crooked. He tried to straighten it, embarrassed under the Commissar's glare.

"Do you know him?"

"Maurice? Of course I know him. He's Tekla Kuritsa's son, he teaches in the ridna shkola, and tutors children—for free."

"Goddammit, you liar! This man told me himself he was in UPA. Guards, take him out and shoot him."

Maurice felt cold. His leg began to ache where he had been wounded at Kiev, and he irrationally feared that the pain would give him away—that the Commissar would be able to take it as proof that he had served in the Army.

"I don't know anything about that," the mayor said, speaking quickly. "I know he's a good man, an intelligent man, loyal. He's never been a nationalist."

"There is no record of him as a teacher before the war," said the commissar.

"We destroyed the records three years ago to keep them out of the Germans' hands," the Mayor said.

"What about you?" asked the commissar. "Are you a Party member?"

"Yes."

"Show me your membership card."

"I destroyed it when the Germans came. They would have shot me. I have daughters, comrade commissar."

The commissar drummed his fingers on the table.

"Listen, please, Commissar," the mayor continued. "This man is not a nationalist. He's not in UPA, not a spy. I personally vouch for him." Maurice wondered how much of his history Husar actually knew.

"Very well. Put him on the train for Donbass."

This time, there was no time to go home and collect any belongings. Maurice and the other captives were loaded onto a battered, creaking train and were soon on their way east, to another training camp.

This time, Maurice was not an officer, but a private soldier. The Red Army would again send him to fight—and probably die—against Nazi Germany.

This is the end of Under the Nazi Heel, *the second part of Maurice Bury's wartime story. Part Three,* Walking Out of War, *will be published in 2016. Turn the page for a preview.*

Preview from Walking Out of War

Donbass training camp, August 1944

"How did you learn to break down a rifle so quickly?" the drill sergeant asked.

"I grew up on a farm," Maurice answered. "You have to have a gun on a farm."

"A shotgun, yes. Not an automatic rifle. I come from a farm, too."

Maurice shrugged, hoping the sergeant would not hear his hammering heart. "I guess I'm just a fast learner."

The sergeant's eyes narrowed, but he moved on to the boy beside Maurice, who was fumbling with his weapon. "Get that magazine back together in the next sixty seconds or you're on double guard duty tonight!"

I have to be more clumsy. And more careful, at the same time, Maurice thought.

Compared to his experience as an officer three years earlier, this training camp for soldiers was brutal. In August 1944, the Red Army had reached the outskirts of Warsaw and was within sight of the Gulf of Riga.

They had pushed the Germans out of Russia, Ukraine and Belorussia and were throwing every man they could find into the drive to destroy Hitler's Germany.

In June, the Red Army had launched Operation Bagration. Two million men, thousands of tanks, heavy assault guns and airplanes, along with 220,000 trucks from the U.S., as well as tanks and guns from Britain, tonnes and tonnes of food and ammunition from the West, attacked in a coordinated series of attacks along a front that stretched from Estonia to Romania. In two months, they pushed the Germans out of Belorussia and moved the battle lines up to 200 miles west.

The Soviets annihilated the German Army Group Center. Hundreds of thousands of German soldiers were killed, wounded and captured, including 31 of the 47 generals of Army Group Center—a quarter of the German strength on the Eastern Front gone in two months.

The Red Army's losses, while not as severe, were still huge: 800,000 casualties, including over 180,000 killed and missing.

In August, the communists put Maurice and other men they had rounded up on a train. Two days later, he found himself in a training camp in the Donbas region, the basin of the river Don, famous for coal production and hot summers.

Three years earlier, Maurice had thought that the drill sergeants in the officers' camp were tough. In the camp for enlisted soldiers, the trainers drove the recruits like demons, trying to make them combat-ready in four weeks.

They went on marches for half a day, running much of the time, or dug holes in the ground for no reason.

Maurice was a little better off than the raw recruits. With his previous officer experience, he knew what the drill sergeants wanted. Sometimes too well.

Most of the new recruits were very young, the last remaining boys from the farms and villages across Ukraine, those unlucky enough to reach their 17th birthdays before the war ended.

Not all were young, though. Old Stepan was in his 40s, and Maurice wondered sometimes if Stepan's story wasn't similar to his own. But Stepan obviously had no experience with weapons or army life, and could not keep up with boys literally half his age.

One very hot day, the sergeant assigned Maurice, Stepan and eight young boys to pull an obsolete, heavy cannon up a hill. They knew better by this time than to grumble. Four boys put leather straps over their shoulders and pulled; Maurice and another got behind to push, leaving Stefan and the remaining boys to pull a wagon of ammunition. With the sun beating down on them and the humidity making every breath a chore, they hauled the massive, ancient gun across a muddy field to the bottom of the hill. The wheels squeaked and stuck, then sank into the mud.

"Get moving, you lazy buggers!" the sergeant yelled. "You think Fritz is going to wait for you to get your lazy asses moving? You'd all be dead a hundred times over by now on the battlefield!"

Maurice wondered if the sergeant had ever been to the battlefield, and decided that, in all likelihood, he had. There was almost no one left in Ukraine or Russia now who hadn't been scarred in some way.

So they pushed and pulled the gun across the mud, trying as much as possible to stay on grass so the wheels wouldn't sink so much into the ground. The sergeant had chosen their route to be as difficult as possible.

Halfway to the hill, the wheels stopped turning. The boys paused barely long enough to determine that the cause was too much mud caked around the axles before the sergeant was screaming at them again to keep moving. "The fucking Germans aren't so polite they'll let you clean up! Your comrades are dying on top of that hill unless you get that gun up there! Get moving, you fucking little girls!" Pushing the cannon became dragging the cannon.

It was nearly noon by the time they got the gun to the top of the low hill. Their uniforms were soaked and caked with dust. All the boys fell onto the ground, exhausted.

"Get up!" said the sergeant. The heat was getting to him, too: his shirt was wet with sweat and he wasn't raising his voice anymore. "The Germans have retreated. Take this gun back to the base."

The boys couldn't help groaning, but the sergeant let that pass. They all stood up wearily and picked up the straps. Only Stepan stayed on the ground.

"Won't you join us, comrade?" the sergeant sneered.

"I can't," Stefan puffed. "I'm worn out."

The sergeant pulled his pistol from its holster. "Get up, you lazy son of a bitch, or I'll shoot you right now!"

Eyes wide, Stepan got up, picked up a box of ammunition and led the troop down the hill.

#

Watch for the publication of Walking Out of War *by the end of 2016.*

Thank you for reading *Under the Nazi Heel*. If you enjoyed the sore, please consider writing a review for Amazon or Goodreads. Sharing your opinion not only boosts this title, it also helps other readers find stories that they'll enjoy reading.

If you haven't read Book 1 in *Walking Out of War*, you can find it and all my other titles on my website, writtenword.ca/wordpress/books-by-scott-bury.

Scott Bury

Acknowledgements

Thanks to Maurice Bury for living this story, for surviving and giving the world a beautiful, wonderful daughter, Roxanne.

Thanks to Roxanne for putting up with my not doing anything but work on this book, and others, for such long hours, days, weeks, months and years.

Thanks also to my beta readers and my proofreader, Joy Lorton, the Typo-Detective editor, for being tough on my writing like no one else ever has been.

Thanks to designer and fellow independent author David C. Cassidy for the striking, beautiful and perfect.

And for advice, input, guidance and general support, I have to thank Bob Nailor, J. Felix, Caleb Pirtle III, Gary Henry, Emily Kimelman, Toby Neal, Barb Drozdowich, DelSheree Gladden, Mohanalakshmi Rajakumar, Seb Kirby, Kathleen Valentine and all the members of Independent Authors International and BestSelling Reads.

And thank you, readers. You're why I do this.

About the author

I am a journalist, editor and novelist based in Ottawa, Canada. After more than 20 years of writing for magazines and newspapers like *Macworld*, the *Financial Post*, *Applied Arts*, *the Globe and Mail* and *Graphic Arts Monthly*, I decided to publish my first writing love, fiction. I published a children's story, Sam, the Strawb Part in 2011 and donated all the proceeds to an autism charity. Later, I published an occult/paranormal short story for grown ups, Dark Clouds.

The Bones of the Earth came out in 2012. You might call it an epic fantasy, but I prefer the term that I made up, historical magic realism.

I followed that in 2013 with *One Shade of Red*, an erotic romantic spoof.

In 2015, I entered the Kindle World of fan fiction,

after being invited to write for Toby Neal's Lei Crime Kindle World and Russell Blake's JET Kindle World. I responded with *Torn Roots* and *Jet: Stealth*, respectively.

The first volume in *Walking Out of War*, *Army of Worn Soles*, hit the shelves in 2014. For a short time, it was #3 in the Military Memoirs in Canada category, behind Canadian supersoldier Cody Mitic's *Unflinching: The Making of a Canadian Sniper*.

Book 3, *Walking Out of War*, will be out by the end of 2016. I promise.

In between writing books and blog posts, I've also helped found an author's cooperative publishing venture, Independent Authors International, and I active in the author's professional association BestSelling Reads.

Let me know what you think, or if you have any questions. Contact me through my website, www.writtenword.ca, my blog, Written Words, and on Twitter @ScottTheWriter.

www.ingramcontent.com/pod-product-compliance
Lightning Source LLC
Chambersburg PA
CBHW061325040426
42444CB00011B/2780